Biofeedback in practice

Longman Applied Psychology
General editor: Philip Feldman

Biofeedback in practice
Douglas Carroll

The social creation of mental illness
Raymond Cochrane

Compulsive gamblers
Mark G. Dickerson

Psychological aspects of pregnancy
Anthony Reading

Institutional care and rehabilitation
Geoffrey Shepherd

Forthcoming:

The Schizophrenias
M. J. Birchwood, P. Green and M. C. Preston

Chemical control of behaviour
Steven Cooper

Clinical psychology of the elderly
A. D. M. Davies and A. G. Crisp

Drink and drinking problems
Clive Eastman

Behavioural medicine
P. G. Harvey and B. Dodd

Methods of changing behaviour
Andrée Liddell

Fears and anxieties
D. C. Rowan and C. Eayrs

Biofeedback in practice

Douglas Carroll

Longman
London and New York

Longman Group Limited
Longman House, Burnt Mill, Harlow
Essex CM20 2JE, England
Associated companies throughout the world

Published in the United States of America
by Longman Inc., New York

First published 1984

British Library Cataloguing in Publication Data
Carroll, Douglas
Biofeedback in practice. – (Longman applied psychology series)
1. Biofeedback training
I. Title
152.1′88 BF319.5.B5

ISBN 0-582-29616-1

Library of Congress Cataloging in Publication Data
Carroll, Douglas.
Biofeedback in practice.

(Longman applied psychology)
Bibliography: p.
Includes index.
1. Medicine, Psychosomatic – Addresses, essays, lectures.
2. Biofeedback training – Addresses, essays, lectures.
I. Title. II. Series. [DNLM: 1. Biofeedback (Psychology) WL 103 C319b]
RC49.C37 1984 616'.001'9 83–9399
ISBN 0–582–29616–1 (U.S.)

Set in 9½/11 pt Linotron 202 Times
Printed in Hong Kong by
Warren Printing Co Ltd

Contents

Editor's preface

In most areas of applied psychology there is no shortage of hardback textbooks many hundreds of pages in length. They give a broad coverage of the total field but rarely in sufficient detail in any one topic for undergraduates, particularly honours students. This is even more true for trainees and professionals in such areas as clinical psychology.

The Longman Applied Psychology series consists of authoritative short books each concerned with a specific aspect of applied psychology. The brief given to the authors of this series was to describe the current state of knowledge in the area, how that knowledge is applied to the solution of practical problems and what new developments of real-life relevance may be expected in the near future. The twelve books which have been commissioned so far are concerned mainly with clinical psychology, defined very broadly. Topics range from gambling to ageing and from the chemical control of behaviour to social factors in mental illness.

The books go into sufficient depth for the needs of students at all levels and professionals yet remain well within the grasp of the interested general reader. A number of groups will find their educational and professional needs or their personal interests met by this series: professional psychologists and those in training (clinical, educational, occupational, etc.); psychology undergraduates; undergraduate students in other disciplines which include aspects of applied psychology (e.g. social administration, sociology, management, and particularly medicine); professionals and trainees in fields outside psychology, but which draw on applications of psychology (doctors of all kinds, particularly psychiatrists and general practitioners, social workers, nurses, particularly psychiatric nurses, counsellors – such as school, vocational and marital – personnel managers).

Finally, members of the general public who have been introduced to a particular topic by the increasing number of well-informed and well-presented newspaper articles and television programmes will be able to follow it up and pursue it in more depth.

Philip Feldman

Acknowledgements

My thanks are due to a number of people who have given generously of their time and skills. I thank my friends and colleagues in the department of psychology, University of Birmingham; I can think of few better working environments. I owe a particular debt of gratitude to Phil Feldman for his encouragement, his editorial advice and, latterly, his patience; he was always on hand when my spirits and energies were flagging. Sue Garvey, Barbara Hudson, Beverley Humphries and Lesley Leigh typed the manuscript; given the character of my handwritten drafts, this was no mean achievement.

To Christopher and Liam

Chapter 1

Introduction

Biofeedback

In the late 1960s a new word entered both scientific and everyday vocabulary – biofeedback. The term, shorthand for biological feedback, denoted a range of new technologies geared to supply individuals with information or feedback about the state of play in various internal bodily systems.

Techniques for monitoring biological activity in human subjects have been around for most of this century, and post-war developments in electronics markedly increased the reliability, versatility and availability of instrumentation. By the 1950s a whole host of internal functions could be measured non-invasively, with recording electrodes or sensors strategically attached to the body surface being the only encumbrance. The electrical output from these attachments was then amplified to give a continuous record of physiological activity. Direct access to this information was restricted to scientists or physicians as recordings were made for diagnosis or research. With biofeedback, however, biological signals were relayed back to the subject in a form that could be easily understood, such as a visual or auditory display. Thus, with biofeedback, individuals could now hear their own muscle tension transformed into a tone that shifted in pitch as muscle tension varied, or could observe the moment-to-moment changes in heart rate by means of a pointer moving over a scale.

The rationale for providing such information to individuals was to enable them to extend their capacities for self-control to internal biological systems. Thus with biofeedback, control might be regained over functions that are usually under self-control, but are poorly controlled in a particular instance, e.g. muscle tension, or more remarkably, biofeedback might allow the self-control of functions that conventionally elude conscious efforts at regulation, e.g. heart rate or blood pressure. These were the possibilities created by biofeedback.

Physiological self-regulation

Certainly there were reasons for suspecting that our capacities for biological control had been sorely underestimated by western scientists. Occasional anecdotal accounts seemed to testify to impressive feats of self-regulation. Indian yogis have been credited with possessing striking abilities in this respect. There are accounts of yogis guiding the temperature of the two sides of one palm in different directions, reducing their heart rates and apparently even stopping the heart altogether for short periods of time.

The American illusionist, Harry Houdini, has also been accredited with some remarkable demonstrations of biological self-control. Houdini could extricate himself from a variety of padlocked chains and handcuffs and a key was essential for his escape. An initial search of his clothes and body never revealed a concealed key as Houdini's trick was to suspend one in his throat. Away from the spectators' gaze, he would regurgitate the key and make his apparently fantastic escape. The amazing feat was not the escape, but the concealment of the key. When an object sticks in the throat, one gags as an automatic reflex. Houdini had learnt to control that reflex by constant practice using a piece of potato suspended from a string. There are other examples from the world of entertainment. The nineteenth-century French music-hall artiste, Le Petomane, built a successful and hilarious act out of his ability to control flatulence. Such were his abilities in this sphere that he could play the French National anthem, *a tergo*, as it were.

Furthermore, the scientific journals have also contained occasional examples of biological self-control. As early as 1885, Tarchanoff described a patient able to accelerate his heart rate voluntarily. By manipulating respiration rate, Tarchanoff was able to discount this as the source of the subject's heart rate increase. West and Savage (1918) and King (1920) recounted similar observations, again with single patients. In 1958, the great Soviet psychologist, Alexander Luria, published an engaging account of a man with a remarkable memory. In addition to his mnemonic abilities, the subject could alter his heart rate by as much as 40 beats per minute, and raise the temperature of one hand while simultaneously lowering the temperature of the other.

Our capacity for biological self-regulation might therefore be greater than we realise, and given the appropriate circumstances for learning, we all might manage the control apparently exercised by one or two individuals. The working assumption was that biofeedback would provide just the right circumstances. It has long been appreciated that the skills which we exhibit in everyday life depend for their acquisition on the availability of feedback. We learn to drive a car, play tennis or thread a needle by means of a continuous and accurate visual feedback of the consequences of our efforts. Without it we would never learn to make the appropriate adjustments in each instance. Biofeedback can be regarded as an extension of that feedback principle into an area in which it is naturally fairly deficient, i.e. internal biological activity. There the outcomes of adjustments are generally hidden from view and normally we cannot see or hear the changes in our heart rate or blood pressure. With biofeedback we can; awareness is made possible.

Early promise

The data were quick to accumulate and consistent in their message that given biofeedback, individuals could achieve control over a wide range of physiological systems. By 1970, voluntary control had been reliably demonstrated over heart rate, blood pressure, skin temperature, brain waves, muscle tension, vasomotor tone, salivation and the electrical conductivity of the skin. Few developments in psychobiology can have had such immediate impact. The implications of being able to regulate one's own biology by simply exercising one's will are clearly immense (see Brown 1974). Enthusiasts were quick to point out the enormous therapeutic potential of biological self-regulation, particularly with regard to stress-related disorders. Biofeedback, they speculated, could provide an alternative to drug-based approaches for a whole range of conditions: hypertension, migraine, tension headaches, cardiac disorders, epilepsy, anxiety and so on. By facilitating the psychological control of physiology, biofeedback would restore to each person the means for determining his or her own health and well-being. While a review of the early laboratory reports (Blanchard and Young 1973) cautioned that the control achieved was almost invariable modest, it was countered that so too was the amount of feedback training provided, and more protracted training would lead to more substantial control. In addition, these early reports had dealt mainly with healthy subjects whose systems were functioning normally, so the scope for modification might have been fairly limited. On the other hand, patients with abnormal levels of activity in a system, might be capable, given biofeedback, of realizing more significant changes.

Ground rules for evaluation

Over a decade has elapsed since the therapeutic implications of biofeedback were first broadcast, and biofeedback has now been applied to a variety of clinical conditions. Has its much publicized potential been realized in practice?

To answer this question, the research in each of the major areas of application must be subjected to careful and critical scrutiny and the ground rules must be laid down for such an evaluation at the outset.

First of all, it is not enough to ask merely if an individual's condition has improved with treatment. This is only a first step and is insufficient to establish efficacy. The therapy may prove to be applicable only to particular individuals, while others may be left as they were. Thus a sizeable number of patients have to be treated successfully before general pronouncements can be made. In additon, patients may improve simply as a function of time. To account for spontaneous recovery, the improvement rate for patients subjected to biofeedback must be compared to the improvement rate of patients suffering from the same disorder but receiving no specific treatment.

Second, it is now widely acknowledged that a treatment can often stimulate improvement through the powerful agency of expecting relief. The novelty of the therapy, its technological sophistication, and the enthusiasm of the therapist all seem to be important in encouraging such so-called placebo effects. It is therefore necessary to establish that biofeedback engenders specific effects and is not merely an elaborate placebo. One way of doing this is to provide, as a check, biofeedback that is independent of the patient's biological functioning i.e. false feedback.

Third, it is always important to compare any new treatment with cheaper and more easily administered alternatives. While, in matters of health care, economic considerations should never be allowed to dictate therapeutic conduct, cost-effectiveness will always be an important factor.

Finally, the patient's condition should be assessed thoroughly and objectively both before and after treatment. As many of the disorders that have been treated by biofeedback are intermittently troublesome, e.g. migraine, or are characterized by day-to-day variation, e.g. high blood pressure, assessment should be carried out over a reasonable period of time. A cursory examination will give an unrepresentative estimate of a patient's condition. Patients should also be subjected to long-term follow-up to ensure that improvement is maintained when biofeedback is withdrawn and the individual is confronted by the stresses of everyday life.

With these considerations in mind, let us examine the clinical research relating to biofeedback.

Chapter 2

Cardiovascular dysfunctions: hypertension

Introduction

One of the first disorders to attract the new biofeedback technology was high blood pressure, or more precisely, essential hypertension. It seemed a sensible choice for several reasons.

First of all, it is a substantial problem. It is estimated that 15 to 20 per cent of the populations of western countries exhibit high blood pressure; world-wide estimates fluctuate around 10 per cent. The term essential hypertension is applied where there is no detectable medical or organic cause, which is the case in the vast majority of instances. While a number of contributory factors have been proposed, recent research (see Obrist 1976) points to the over-riding influence of psychological stress and constitutional susceptibility. Concern with essential hypertension largely reflects its association with heart disease and stroke. The results of various studies testify that, as blood pressure increases, so life expectancy decreases. Since 1949, the small community of Framingham in the USA has been the subject of close medical scrutiny. At the start of the study, some 5,000 of its citizens had their blood pressures taken, and about 20 per cent of them had blood pressure in the hypertensive range. Kannel (1977) reviewed their subsequent medical progress and found that individuals with high blood pressure were three times more likely to have suffered heart attacks, six times more likely to have had congestive heart failure and eight times more likely to have suffered strokes than those with blood pressures in the normal range.

Second, there was and still is dissatisfaction with existing drug treatments for hypertension. Some patients do not respond well to antihypertensive medication, while others experience undesirable side effects which can be sufficiently disturbing to cause patients to abandon their medication. Finally, antihypertensive drugs only manage high blood pressure, they do not cure it and the treatment must be maintained throughout the patient's life.

Third, it had already been demonstrated that individuals with normal blood pressure levels could, when given biofeedback, raise and lower blood pressure reliably (e.g. Shapiro, et al. 1969); Shapiro, et al. 1970; Brener and Kleinman, 1970). While the alterations were modest, so too were the training schedules; usually only one session of feedback had been provided. The results certainly held out the promise that given the benefit of more extensive biofeedback training, patients with excessively high levels of blood pressure, would be able to effect clinically significant changes.

Blood pressure measurement and biofeedback

Blood pressure is a function of the force with which the heart ejects blood into the arterial circulatory system and the resistance offered by that system to the passage of blood. Since blood is expelled from the heart in discrete pulses, pressure will vary during the heart's cycle of activity. When the heart is in its active or systolic phase, pressure will be at a maximum as the ventricle chambers contract and forcibly eject blood into the arteries. On the other hand, pressure will be at a minimum during the heart's passive or diastolic phase. Accordingly, blood pressure is described by two numbers; the highest is the pressure during the heart's systolic phase, i.e. systolic pressure (SBP), while the lower figure signifies pressure during the diastolic phase, i.e. diastolic pressure (DBP). In both cases, pressure is measured in millimetres of mercury (mmHg). In essential hypertension, both pressures are excessively high. While definitions of what is 'high' vary slightly, pressures above 150/90 mmHg are generally considered excessive. The average blood pressure of young adults sitting quietly is approximately 125/75 mmHg. The raised pressures of essential hypertension stem mainly from an increase in peripheral resistance. Because of this the heart must labour harder to circulate blood and it is this extra load which increases the risk of heart disease and stroke.

Blood pressure is readily amenable to indirect measurement. An inflatable cuff is wrapped around the upper arm and then connected to a manometer and a hand pump with a valve. It is inflated to a pressure above the individual's likely SBP, the valve is then opened, and the pressure in the cuff allowed to drop slowly. SBP is determined by listening with a stethoscope placed on the brachial artery below the cuff. Korotkoff sounds (described as hissing, clicking or gurgling) will be detected when the cuff pressure equals the individual's SBP and flow in the brachial artery is no longer totally occluded. The pressure at this point can be read in mmHg from the manometer. These Korotkoff sounds disappear eventually when the cuff pressure is allowed to drop sufficiently for arterial flow to be restored completely. The manometer reading at this point allows the DBP to be determined.

While this method of measurement is perfectly satisfactory for an occasional check on blood pressure, it is not suitable for continuous and immediate biofeedback. However, the cuff procedure can be modified and automated to give the patient access to blood pressure on each beat of the heart. In the most widely adopted technique, the cuff is automatically inflated to the subject's average resting SBP and held there. Whenever the SBP rises and exceeds the cuff pressure, blood will be forced through the artery under the cuff, resulting in a Korotkoff sound which can be detected electronically rather than with a stethoscope. On the other hand, for those heart beats where the SBP is less than the occluding pressure of the cuff, blood flow will be prevented and there will be no attendant Korotkoff sound. Thus, this system yields information on the relative status of SBP (indicating if it is above or below the average) on each successive heart beat. This is then easily relayed to the patient as continuous, binary feedback of either relatively high or, more pertinently, relatively low pressures on each heart beat. The procedure can also be used for DBP biofeedback. Here the cuff pressure is set initially at the average resting DBP, with binary feedback provided for the absence of Korotkoff sounds. In either case, cuff pressure can be reset on successive trials as progressively lower pressures are achieved.

Biofeedback efficacy

Benson, et al. (1971) reported the first clinical study in this context. Although seven patients were studied, only five had been diagnosed as having essential hypertension. After five to sixteen daily sessions had established baseline blood pressure levels, SBP biofeedback was provided using the method just described. The number of daily sessions of feedback varied from 8 to 34; the mean was 22. Each session lasted about an hour. The results indicated that, on average, SBP decreased from 165 mmHg during the last 5 baseline sessions to 148 mmHg during the last 5 biofeedback sessions. However, only the five patients suffering from essential hypertension responded positively to treatment; these five showed overall decreases in SBP of 16–34 mmHg over training sessions. For the other two patients, no reliable reductions in pressure were recorded. While these results are encouraging, unqualified assertions of efficacy would be premature. First of all, since Benson et al. failed to check blood pressure outside the laboratory and collected no systematic follow-up data, the general and lasting effectiveness of their treatment remains to be established. In fact, casual follow-up of these patients (see Blanchard 1979) revealed that SBP tended to revert to pretreatment levels within a few months of treatment. Second, in the absence of any comparison condition (patients receiving either no treatment or a control treatment), it is difficult to attribute the changes in SBP unequivocably to biofeedback. Regular periods of merely sitting, or the placebo effects of a new treatment and impressive instrumentation, readily spring to mind as alternative explanations.

Miller (1972, 1975) presented results on a single patient selected from a group of 28 essential hypertensives initially treated with DBP biofeedback. While, in general, response to the treatment varied considerably, this particular patient displayed reductions in DBP sufficiently impressive to merit more extensive training. In total, thirty-seven sessions of biofeedback were provided over three months and the DBP fell to 76 mmHg from a baseline of 97 mmHg. Again, caution is warranted. Although checks in the ward suggested that the training effects had generalized even with medication suspended, the patient subsequently redeveloped hypertension after re-exposure to life stresses.

Schwartz and Shapiro (1973) also decided to concentrate on DBP. After five sessions of baseline recording, seven hypertensive patients were exposed in turn to three conditions: in the first, they were instructed simply to 'think pleasant thoughts and relax'; in the second condition DBP biofeedback was provided along with financial rewards for pressure reductions; in the final condition, subjects received feedback for increasing as well as for lowering DBP. There were five daily sessions in each condition. The results however, revealed no overall changes in DBP relative to baseline in any of the three conditions. The average baseline DBP was 102 mmHg, and average values of 104, 102 and 102 mmHg were recorded for the three conditions respectively. Only one of the seven patients achieved anything approaching a satisfactory decrease; for that individual DBP fell to 85 mmHg from a 99 mmHg baseline. However, without follow-up data, the durability of even that single success must remain open to doubt.

None of the studies discussed so far employed experimental designs that establish biofeedback unambiguously as the key factor in any resultant blood pressure changes. In addition, none included any formal follow-up. In an attempt to remedy this, Elder, et al. (1973) allocated eighteen hypertensive patients to one of three treatment groups. Following a session devoted to assessing baseline pressures, the first group had their pressures monitored and were instructed to relax and to try to lower their blood pressure without the aid of biofeedback. After the baseline session, the second group was given DBP biofeedback to facilitate decreases in pressure, while the final group received social feedback, i.e. praise, in addition to the biofeedback. Praise was regulated to coincide with success; patients were told 'good' when DBP first fell below the criterion, 'very good' if it fell 5 mmHg below and 'wonderful' if it dropped 10 mmHg below. For each of the groups, seven sessions of treatment were provided over a period of four days.

From the analysis of the three groups' performances, it was apparent that this biofeedback plus social feedback group was consistently more successful at lowering DBP than the other two groups. By the final sessions, the average DBP of this group was 80 per cent that recorded at baseline. In addition, the group given only biofeedback ultimately registered a lower DBP than the group not provided with biofeedback. These effects were maintained at follow-up a week after the final session, when the biofeedback plus social feedback group had an average DBP of some 19 mmHg below baseline. While the biofeedback-alone group was not quite as responsive it still fared better than the group without feedback. Changes in SBP generally parallelled those for DBP, with the biofeedback plus social feedback group showing the most emphatic reductions (a drop of 23 mmHg between baseline and follow-up). It is a pity that Elder et al. did not include a longer follow-up, and that only one session of baseline measurement was employed. It is important to have well-established, stable baselines before treatment (Shapiro et al. 1977). DBP is subject to a good deal of variation. In particular, levels may be a typically high during initial periods of laboratory measurement and decline as patients become accustomed to laboratory conditions. Thus, insufficient baseline assessment would favour the appearance of subsequent decreases in pressure.

In a later study, Elder and Eustis (1975) did manage a more long term follow-up. As before, though, only one session was allowed for baseline assessment. Twenty-two patients were given twenty sessions of DBP biofeedback but no social feedback was provided. The results were much less impressive than those reported previously. The average reduction in DBP was less than 10 per cent, with only nine patients out of the twenty-two showing reliable decreases. SBP fell by only 8 mmHg on average and the DBP by 7 mmHg. A follow-up of selected patients over a month later could find no long-term gains from biofeedback treatment. It is perhaps unfortunate that Elder and Eustis did not persevere with social feedback in combination with biofeedback; it was easily the most effective treatment in the earlier study.

Blanchard et al. (1975) also offer some follow-up data. Four patients were provided with intermittent SBP biofeedback using a simple alternative to the usual arrangement. SBP was determined once a minute using the cuff technique, and plotted by the experimenter on a graph made clearly visible to the patient. Patients completed four sessions of baseline assessment and received between five and thirteen sessions of feedback. Given the simplicity of the biofeedback technique; the results would seem particularly encouraging. The overall average decrease in SBP was 26 mmHg. While the initial baselines of these four patients ranged from 144 to 182 mmHg, their average levels with biofeedback ranged from 117 to 135 mmHg. At follow-up one week after treatment, one patient registered a SBP of 129 mmHg, 53 mmHg below the initial baseline value. At two-week follow-up, a second patient exhibited a systolic pressure of 125 mmHg, 17 mmHg below baseline. While these data are certainly impressive, scientific rigour requires more complete and extended follow-up information. In addition, it should be mentioned that only one of Blanchard et al.'s patients was properly hypertensive; the other three displayed only borderline hypertension. The high but variable pressures that characterize borderline hypertension are not always consolidated into the more rigidly high pressures of hypertension proper.

It is generally considered that Kristt and Engel (1975) offered the most persuasive evidence for biofeedback as a lasting treatment in cases of essential hypertension. Five patients with long histories of essential hypertension were studied, but full data were available only for four of them. The experiment comprised three phases. In phase 1, the patients monitored their own baseline blood pressure four times daily for at least five weeks and posted the results to the investigators. In phase 2, they were admitted to hospital and given biofeedback training for three weeks, receiving approximately fourteen sessions per week. During the first week they were provided with biofeedback for raising SBP. Throughout the second week, training was geared to reductions in SBP, while the third week was given over alternatively to raising and lowering pressure. For phase 3, the patients were taught how to administer the feedback procedure themselves, provided with the apparatus, and instructed to practise as regularly as possible at home. On average, they practised between four and thirty times daily for three months and again mailed in the results of their effort. Their abilities were also evaluated twice in hosptial during this period.

All four patients for whom there were complete data were successful at reducing SBP in the hospital. By the end of phase 2, their overall average SBP had fallen to 144 mmHg from a baseline of 162 mmHg. DBP had also fallen; this time to 87 mmHg from 95 mmHg. In addition, these gains were maintained at home with regular home practice; SBP decreased even further to around 125 mmHg. Finally, as a result of biofeedback training, three of Kristt and Engel's patients were able to reduce substantially their reliance on antihypertensive drugs.

In sharp contrast to Kristt and Engel, Shoemaker and Tasto (1975) could find no evidence at all for biofeedback. Fifteen hypertensive patients were allocated to one of three conditons. Following three baseline sessions, the five patients in one condition practised progressive relaxation for six sessions over a period of two weeks. Progressive relaxation involves individuals vigorously tensing particular groups of muscles before relaxing them as much as possible. This procedure of tensing followed by relaxing is applied progressively throughout the body. A second group of five patients were instructed to decrease blood pressure and given intermittent biofeedback (once every 90 seconds) of both SBP and DBP, again for six sessions. The final group of patients spent a similar amount of time in the laboratory and had their blood pressures monitored but received no formal training. Overall, only the relaxation group demonstrated changes in pressure. On average SBP decreased by 7 mmHg and DBP by 8 mmHg. The biofeedback treatment was completely ineffective. However, given the character of the feedback provision, this was perhaps not wholly unexpected. Shoemaker and Tasto relied on a series of mirrors to reveal the polygraph chart on which pressure levels were intermittently recorded. It is doubtful whether any useful information about blood pressure could have been conveyed to patients by such a crude arrangement.

It is a great pity that Shoemaker and Tasto's feedback facility was so feeble, given the inclusion of no-treatment and alternative treatment groups for comparison. Only one of the studies reported so far bothered with what are, in fact, critical requirements for an unambiguous determination of efficacy. Fortunately nearly all of the most recent research is much better in this respect. Follow-up assessment has also become much more usual.

Goldman, et al. (1975), for example, included a control group who were told merely to relax as much as possible; for these four hypertensive patients blood pressure was monitored but no biofeedback was given. The experimental group of seven hypertensives, on the other hand, received nine weekly sessions of SBP biofeedback. Comparisons between readings taken at the beginning of sessions 1 and 9, indicated that, for the biofeedback group, SBP had decreased reliably, although unspectacularly, from 167 mmHg to 161 mmHg; DBP, however, had dropped substantially more, from 109 mmHg to 94 mmHg. Analogous measurements for the control group revealed no consistent changes; while the average initial pressure was 155/99 mmHg, the average final pressure was 157/95 mmHg. Although no follow-up was reported in this instance, Kleinman, et al. (1977) presented follow-up data on a subsequent group of eight patients exposed to the same biofeedback treatment, preceded this time, however, by three sessions of baseline assessment. Following the last feedback session, patients monitored their own blood pressures daily at home for four months, although by the end of four months data were available for only three of the patients. The results indicated that blood pressures decreased significantly in the clinic: from 151/94 mmHg before treatment to 143/85 mmHg during the last two sessions of biofeedback. Reductions of around the same order were registered outside the clinic: from 155/97 mmHg one day before the last two baseline sessions to 147/89 mmHg before the last two feedback sessions. These effects were reported to persist to some extent after treatment had finished; SBP remained below 150 mmHg and DBP below 90 mmHg.

Walsh et al. (1977) re-examined the relative merits of biofeedback and progressive relaxation in the treatment of hypertension. In phase one of their study, twenty-four essential hypertensives were allocated to either a biofeedback or a progressive relaxation condition. The biofeedback group received continuous feedback, not of blood pressure this time, but of pulse wave velocity. The latter is measured as the transit time, i.e. the time elapsing from the beat of the heart to the arrival of the ensuing pressure wave at some peripheral point, such as the wrist. Transit time is inversely related to the velocity of the wave, i.e. pulse wave velocity, which is in turn related directly to blood pressure. The advantages of this technique over the standard cuff method are increased patients' comfort and the option of providing analogue feedback. The main disadvantage is that pulse wave velocity cannot be scaled in mmHg. Cuff measurements are still essential to check absolute pressure levels. Twelve patients were given continuous biofeedback of pulse wave velocity and instructed to reduce blood pressure for five weekly sessions, while the remaining twelve spent a similar amount of time practising progressive relaxation. In phase 2, sixteen patients (eight from each phase 1 condition) received further training with both biofeedback and progressive relaxation, again for five weekly sessions. Inspection of the graphs presented by Walsh et al. indicates that by the end of phase 1, the biofeedback group demonstrated much more substantial reductions in blood pressure than the relaxation group; while blood pressure for the former dropped on average from around 151/94 to 129/81 mmHg, for the latter it decreased from around 142/94 to 135/88 mmHg. By the beginning of phase 2, however, pressures had increased somewhat and the subsequent combined treatment appeared to be less effective than biofeedback alone. For the original biofeedback patients, pressure changed from around 138/83 at the beginning of phase 2 to around 131/85 mmHg at the end. For the relaxation patients, a similar average change was recorded: from around 143/87 to 137/89 mmHg. At the three-month follow-up, the biofeedback and relaxation groups registered around 133/84 and 147/91 mmHg respectively, while at follow-up a year after treatment, the biofeedback group displayed an overall average pressure of 135/84 and the relaxation group a remarkably similar average pressure of 133/85 mmHg. Thus, compared to the initial pretreatment overall average of 146/94 mmHg, the final overall average of 134/85 represents reasonable progress. However, such long-term gains can hardly be attributed with complete confidence to biofeedback, since both groups displayed similar average pressures at one year follow-up. Admittedly, the biofeedback group had higher pressures to start with than the relaxation group and were doing noticeably better before the introduction of the combined treatment.

In a study focussing on borderline hypertension Surwit et al. (1978) also compared biofeedback with other modes of treatment, but with decidely less success. Twenty-four borderline hypertensives were assigned to one of three equally-sized groups. Group 1 received biofeedback for simultaneous reductions in blood pressure and heart rate. Group 2 were also given biofeedback, but this time, for combined reductions in muscle tension, i.e. electromyographic activity, in the forearm extensor and forehead frontalis muscles. The final group were instructed to relax and meditate, using a technique similar in many respects to transcendental meditation. Following two baseline sessions, patients received eight sessions of their allotted treatment. Follow-up assessments were undertaken six weeks and a year after treatment, although only thirteen patients were available for final assessment. Overall, SBP showed only the most marginal change across sessions, from 140 mmHg to 137 mmHg. There were no reliable differences among the three treatment groups. At six-week follow-up the average SBP was only 6 mmHg less than that recorded at the beginning of the first training session and DBP was only 3 mmHg less. By final follow-up, both the average SBP and DBP had actually risen by some 3 mmHg over that exhibited at six weeks.

Blanchard et al. (1977) also compared blood pressure

biofeedback with electromyographic feedback. Following four sessions of baseline assessment, thirty hypertensives were assigned randomly to one of three groups. Group 1 received intermittent blood pressure biofeedback, using the technique developed by Blanchard et al. (1975) and described previously. Group 2 were given electromyographic feedback: this time from the forehead site only. The third group of ten patients were instructed simply to relax and to try and lower blood pressure without the aid of feedback. In all, there were twelve sessions of treatment, and follow-up evaluations were carried out four times within the first two weeks and then at six, ten, and fourteen weeks following treatment. Results revealed no reliable differences among the three treatments and only very modest overall treatment effects. The average drop in blood pressure from baseline to early follow-up was 6.5 mmHg for SBP and 2.0 mmHg for DBP. Thus, in line with Surwit et al, biofeedback appeared to be only marginally effective and no more effective than relaxation achieved by the simplest of instructions.

Friedman and Taub (1977, 1978) compared intermittent biofeedback of DBP with relaxation induced through hypnosis and combined hypnosis and biofeedback. The hypnosis-alone procedure elicited the highest and most sustained reductions in pressure. The biofeedback-alone group came a poor second, while the combined treatment group showed no reliable changes throughout. From baseline to the last training session, SBP and DBP dropped by 13 and 9 mmHg respectively for the hypnosis group, by 8 and 6 mmHg respectively for the biofeedback group, 1 and 2 mmHg respectively for the combined group and 3 and 4 mmHg for a measurement-only control group. The picture was largely the same one week and one month after treatment. At the earlier follow-up, the average SBP and DBP decreases from baseline were 13 and 10 mmHg respectively for the hypnosis group, 7 and 7 mmHg for the biofeedback group, 2 and 3 mmHg for the combined group and 2 and 2 mmHg for the control group. At the later follow-up, the analogous changes were 11 and 7 mmHg, 9 and 3 mmHg, 0 and 6 mmHg for the three treatment conditions respectively. For the measurement-only control condition, SBP was actually marginally higher (2 mmHg) at one month, whereas DBP decreased by the same magnitude.

The results of Walsh et al. and Friedman and Taub strongly imply that a combined treatment package of relaxation plus biofeedback represents a particularly ineffective approach to combatting hypertension. As such, they contrast sharply with the findings of Patel using a mixture of biofeedback and relaxation techniques derived from yoga. In the first of two controlled studies (Patel 1975) forty hypertensives were allocated to one of two equally-sized groups. The experimental group received biofeedback for increases in skin resistance (since the skin resistance of the hands decreases sharply under conditions of stress, an increase in resistance can be regarded as reflecting a shift towards a less aroused, more relaxed state). In addition, these patients were encouraged to relax via a series of exercises derived mainly from yoga relaxation and meditation practices. Patients were instructed to concentrate on smooth breathing, repeat the word 'relax' on each expiration, and to focus mentally on various parts of the body, rendering them flaccid and relaxed. Training continued for three months with approximately three sessions per week. Patients in the control group attended for the same amount of time but merely rested quietly; they received neither biofeedback nor guidance regarding relaxation. Baseline blood pressure was assessed during three sessions for each group. The results were clear cut; while the blood pressures of patients in the control condition remained unchanged throughout, dramatic reductions were evident for the experimental group of patients. On average, pressure for this group fell from a baseline of 159/100 mgHg to 139/86 by the end of training. Follow-up at three, six, nine and twelve months indicated that the gains had been maintained. In addition, the levels of antihypertensive medication were able to be reduced substantially for twelve of the twenty experimental patients; they were still on reduced dosages at twelve month follow-up.

A subsequent study by Patel and North (1975) found much the same sort of effect, but with less extensive training. Thirty-four hypertensive patients took part in this study and were again assigned to one of two groups. As before, the experimental group received a mixture of biofeedback and yoga relaxation exercises. However, only twelve sessions of training were undertaken this time, and in the later sessions, biofeedback of electromyographic activity was introduced as an alternative to skin resistance feedback. The control group received twelve sessions of resting quietly. While blood pressure fell impressively for the experimental patients by 26 mmHg (SBP) and 15 mmHg (DBP), the control group showed much less spectacular reductions: 9 mmHg and 5 mmHg respectively. Assessment three months after treatment indicated that while blood pressure had risen somewhat for the experimental group (from 141/84 to 149/88 mmHg), it was still substantially lower than baseline, and had increased decidely less than for the control group (from 160/99 to 177/104 mmHg). Finally, at the end of this study, the control group patients were given twelve sessions of the biofeedback and relaxation treatment. Although largely unresponsive in their previous, resting quietly sessions, they now showed marked reductions in pressure. SBP fell on average by 28 mmHg and DBP on average by 15 mmHg.

More recently, Patel et al. (1981) have produced further evidence for the effectiveness of this treatment package. Fifty hypertensives, most of whom were not on medication, were treated with this combination of biofeedback, relaxation and yoga. A further forty-three hypertensives served as no-treatment controls. With treatment, SBP dropped by 20 mmHg on average, and DBP by 11 mmHg; these gains were still evident at follow-up six months later. The no-treatment control group displayed only a marginal reduction in blood pressure. These results for unmedicated hypertensives represent important confirmation of the value of Patel's method. Many of the patients treated in the earlier series were on some form of antihypertensive medication. It is always possible in such circumstances that the treatment worked mainly because it increased the regularity with which patients took their medication; after all, some hypertensives have been reported to show poor compliance with medication.

While Patel's results are certainly impressive, it is difficult to ascertain the active ingredient(s) in this rather complex treatment package. However, there is evidence from another source that the major effects may have been produced by the yoga exercises rather than biofeedback. Datey, et al. (1969) trained a group of forty-seven hypertensives in the yoga exercise of 'shavasan' for three weeks and asked them to continue practising the technique afterwards. The exercise involves relaxation and breathing manipulations similar to those used by Patel. In terms of existing treatment, three medication groups could be discerned: a group of ten, not on drugs; a group of twenty-two whose blood pressure was well-controlled by drugs; and a group of fifteen whose blood pressure was not being managed adequately by anti-hypertensive medication. For the first group, the continued practice of 'shavasan' effected a drop in mean pressure (the average of SBP and DBP) from 134 to 107 mmHg. Since the second group already registered an acceptable average mean pressure of 102 mmHg with medication, efforts concentrated on trying to reduce drug dosage. With no rise in pressure, drug dosage was able to be reduced to a third of its initial level in thirteen patients. A similar reduction was effected in six of the final group.

Finally, Luborsky et al. (1982) compared SBP biofeedback with antihypertensive medication. Patients with mild hypertension were allocated to one of four treatment groups: ten patients were prescribed medication (usually a diuretic), sixteen were trained in progressive relaxation, eleven performed a series of physical exercises, and fourteen received SBP biofeedback for a total of fifteen sessions. Only the medication group displayed impressive reductions in blood pressure with treatment; blood pressure fell from an initial average of 144/97 to 128/88 mmHg. The average changes for the other three groups were as follows: for the relaxation group blood pressure fell by 7/4 mmHg, for the exercise group it fell by 3/2 mmHg, and for the SBP biofeedback group it fell by 5/5 mmHg.

Conclusions

Overall these studies offer neither consistent nor unambiguous support for the application of biofeedback to essential hypertension. While most of them bear witness to reductions in blood pressure with biofeedback, a significant number report only marginal effects or none at all. In addition, many of the more encouraging results are compromised by methodological weaknesses. Often, for example, follow-up data has been either absent, incomplete or of insufficient duration. Only just over a handful of the studies focussing on blood pressure biofeedback have included assessment a month or longer after treatment. Of these, less than a half indicate sustained reductions in pressure. The persistent failure to control fully for the passage of time (by including a no-treatment comparison condition and ensuring sufficient baseline assessment) let alone the likely placebo effects of a new and technologically impressive treatment, make it difficult to attribute pressure changes to biofeedback with any confidence. Generally it would seem to be the case that where such controls are attempted, so the indications for biofeedback *per se* or relative to other, simpler modes of treatment, diminish considerably (Blanchard et al 1977; Friedman and Taub 1977, 1978; Surwit et al 1978). Apart from Kristt and Engel (1975), the most encouraging data are those reported by Patel (Patel, 1975; Patel and North, 1975), using biofeedback of skin resistance and electromyographic activity rather than blood pressure. However, there is good reason to believe that biofeedback was not the critical element in Patel's treatment package. Even Kristt and Engel's results are susceptible to alternative interpretation; it could be argued that biofeedback worked only in so far as it inclined patients to adopt strategies for relaxation similar to those formally exploited by Patel, and by Datey et al. (1969).

Chapter 3

Cardiovascular dysfunctions: cardiac arrhythmias and circulatory problems

Biofeedback has been applied also to other areas of cardiovascular pathology, in particular to cardiac arrhythmias and Raynaud's disease. Although neither has received anywhere near as much attention as hypertension, there has been sufficient study to provide at least preliminary indications of efficacy. Let us consider the evidence.

Cardiac arrhythmias

The two main cardiac irregularities which have received the most attention are premature ventricular contractions (PVCs) and tachycardia. PVCs are discharges of the ventricles that occur too soon in the heart's cycle of activity, caused by part of the ventricles becoming irritated and triggering an unexpected, early contraction. PVCs occur in about 5 per cent of the adult population, and while an isolated PVC is of little immediate concern, if they occur often and the ventricles contract irregularly and ineffectively they can precipitate cardiac arrest. Tachycardia is when the heart rate is very fast as a result of a variety of abnormalities. Tachycardia can lead to fibrillation, when the heart beats so rapidly that diastole is not long enough for the ventricles to fill up completely and the loss of efficiency can lead to heart failure.

A number of studies have explored the use of heart rate (HR) biofeedback in the treatment of PVCs and tachycardia. Unlike blood pressure, HR is readily accessible to continuous measurement, using the principles of electrocardiology. The action of the heart, like that of any other muscular organ, is associated with measurable changes in electrical potential, and as the body fluids are good conductors, these fluctuations can be detected on the body surface by strategically placed metal electrodes. Following suitable amplification, the electrical changes of the cardiac cycle can be displayed on an oscilloscope or, more usually, on a chart. The typical electrocardiogram waveform is described by the letters PQRST, where the most salient feature of the complex, the R-wave, represents the contraction of the ventricles. With additional circuitry the time between successive R-waves can be measured and converted mathematically to give the heart rate at each successive heart beat. These beat-to-beat changes in HR can then be used to provide either binary or analogue continuous biofeedback.

Premature ventricular contractions

Weiss and Engel (1971) reported the first study of PVCs. Eight patients, whose histories indicated 10–20 PVCs per minute as well as instances of heart failure, were given extensive treatment with binary HR biofeedback. In all, they were exposed to between twenty-two and fifty-three sessions of training, with between one and three sessions daily. Training comprised four phases. In phase 1, following an initial session to determine baseline HR levels, biofeedback was given to promote increases in HR. In phase 2, patients received feedback for HR slowing, while in phase 3, they were trained in raising and lowering HR alternatively. For the final phase, biofeedback was provided for keeping HR within a specified range. Two other features of this last phase are important; first of all, patients were also given feedback when PVCs occurred and second, biofeedback was faded out gradually as HR stabilization developed.

All patients developed some degree of HR control and more importantly, there was a marked reduction in the rates of PVCs to less than 1 per minute during training in five out of the eight patients. Independent evalutions in the ward confirmed these as general reductions in four of the five patients, and follow-up assessments from three to twenty-one months after treatment indicated that the gains had been maintained for all four. Taken at face value, these results commend the application of HR biofeedback for patients with PVCs. However, as indicated earlier, it is difficult in uncontrolled studies to determine precisely the effective treatment component. In fact, in the Weiss and Engel study, there are reasons for suspecting that expectancy of relief and general placebo effects were more important than any specific contribution from the HR biofeedback. First of all, reductions in PVCs appeared at different phases of training in different patients. For two of the patients, the major reduction occurred during phase 3; for two others, the final phase proved optimal and for the fifth there was a significant decrease in PVCs during HR slowing, with further improvement during phase 3. If feedback was the crucial element, we would expect a more uniform course of improvement. Second, there was on the other hand a strong relationship between improvement and the number of sessions undertaken with a particular patient; those given the most therapeutic attention displayed the most benefit.

It would be wrong to underestimate the power of non-specific placebo effects in this context. Beecher (1961) provided a good example of the placebo at work in cardiac pathology. Evidently, a particular surgical operation for the relief of angina pectoris (a cardiac condition associated with intense pain) was subsequently discredited as being of no direct relevance to the condition. However, many of the patients who underwent this bogus procedure indicated complete relief from pain. Beecher also reported that the rate of relief was directly related to the surgeon's enthusiasm for the procedure.

Engel and Bleecker (1974) reported on a subsequent patient exposed to much the same regime of HR biofeedback treatment. Baseline assessment revealed a PVC rate of around 15 per minute. The patient mastered the various aspects of HR control in the laboratory and PVCs decreased to less than 1 per minute during training for maintaining HR within a specified range. Follow-up revealed continuing improvement, which was corroborated by 10 hours of electrocardiograph measurement outside the laboratory. While this result is again impressive, the outcome cannot be attributed unequivocally to the effects of HR biofeedback *per se*.

Pickering and Gorham (1975) used HR biofeedback to treat a patient whose rate of PVCs depended on HR level. The rate evidently varied between zero and 15 per minute, with the highest rates evident in conditions that elevate HR (circumstances producing emotional tension, following stimulants like coffee, etc.). The patient was given sixteen sessions of HR biofeedback over a period of six weeks and was, as a result, able both to increase and decrease HR. Thus, when PVCs occurred in the laboratory, the patient was able to reduce HR sufficiently to check their occurrence. In addition, training seemed to effect an increase in the HR threshold at which PVCs appeared, from 79 to 94 beats per minute. So Pickering and Gorham lend further support for biofeedback in the context of cardiac arrhythmias; it is a pity, though, that they undertook no follow-up and, accordingly, left open to doubt the durability of the effects.

Pickering and Miller (1977) reported briefly on two other patients with PVCs. Both received fairly extensive HR control training with biofeedback, followed by feedback of normal and PVC heart beats. While one of the patients demonstrated reliable control of the arrhythmia both with and without biofeedback, the other was successful only in the presence of feedback; control was lost when feedback was removed. Again, there was no follow-up evaluation.

Finally, Lown et al. (1976) treated a patient with PVCs who had suffered previous cardiac arrest. The patient was instructed to meditate twice daily and to try to decrease the PVCs by informal feedback of his cardiac activity. Although PVCs decreased from a maximum of 7 per minute to zero by the time of discharge from hospital, it is difficult to attribute this improvement to the overall behavioural treatment package, let alone the biofeedback component of it, since training onset coincided with the start of anti-arrhythmia medication. The patient was free of PVCs at follow-up, nine months after discharge. Again, however, the origins of the sustained improvement are unclear; the patient still regularly practised meditation, and was still receiving arrhythmia medication.

Tachycardia

In addition to their PVC patient, Engel and Bleecker (1974) also reported on two patients exhibiting tachycardia. Following one session for baseline determination, the first patient was given twenty-five sessions of biofeedback to facilitate reductions in HR. HR did, in fact, decrease across training sessions; by the final session it was 105 beats per minute, compared to a baseline level of 116 beats per minute. Independent measurement indicated that this decrease had generalized outside the laboratory. Although follow-up at three weeks revealed rather variable HR levels, ranging from 60 beats per minute in some instances to between 120 and 160 in others, at five-month follow-up HR was stable between 60 and 75 beats per minute. The second patient was trained to decrease HR for 21 daily sessions. Binary HR biofeedback was provided as before, but was gradually faded out in later sessions. The patient's history indicated an initial resting HR level of around 106 beats per minute; it had never fallen below 80 beats per minute during 50 observations taken over 40 years. With training, HR dropped from 86 to 68 beats per minute and this improvement was sustained outside the laboratory. During weekly visits to a doctor, HR was generally around 75 beats per minute. However, no long-term follow-up was reported.

Scott, Blanchard et al. (1973) also reported on two tachycardia patients. After four sessions had established baseline HR levels, the first patient received 53 sessions of treatment which included HR biofeedback to aid HR lowering as well as access to television after successful HR reductions. With training, HR dropped from 89 to 72 beats per minute, a level well within the normal range, and the patient was improved sufficiently to return to work. At 18-month follow-up, the patient was still in employment and had managed to reduce his reliance on tranquillizers. Following the same period of baseline assessment, the second patient was given similar, if less extensive, training. Thirty sessions were undertaken this time, and during the first part of the training HR decreased from 96 to 84 beats per minute; by the end of training, it had stabilized at around 78 beats per minute, an overall drop of 18 beats per minute. Unfortunately, no long-term follow-up data are available for this patient. Further, for neither of the patients is there any report of HR levels outside the laboratory. Scott, Peters, et al. (1973) described another tachycardia patient subjected to analogous treatment, with the addition of a final condition where access to television was contingent on increases in HR. With biofeedback to facilitate HR lowering, HR fell from 87 to 71 beats per minute and remained low in a subsequent no-feedback condition. However, with the HR increase contingency, HR rose again to pretreatment levels. Again there were no follow-up data on cardiac functioning.

The research on HR biofeedback and cardiac arrhythmias is still at a fairly early stage of development, consisting entirely of single or multiple case studies, which, while interesting and provocative in the main, are insufficient to resolve completely the issue of efficacy. Nevertheless, the work of Engel and his associates on PVCs has many sound features, including protracted follow-up assessment, and the sustained improvements recorded for many patients certainly suggest that further research should be undertaken. Thus, a verdict of promising, but as yet unproven, would seem the appropriate one.

Circulatory problems: Raynaud's disease

Let us move now from the centre of the cardiovascular system to the periphery. Most of us have experienced cold hands or feet at one time or another, but for individuals with Raynaud's disease, cold hands and/or feet constitute a chronic problem. In such cases, the arteries of the extremities spasmodically contract, causing a severe reduction or even a cessation of blood flow. The hands and/or feet become pale, insensitive to touch and difficult to move. The condition is usually provoked by exposure to cold but may sometimes be triggered by emotional stress. The symptoms may persist for hours, unless external heat is applied directly to the affected areas. During recovery, the extremities become red and painful. The reaction of normal hands to an over-prolonged snowball fight provide the nearest analogy in common experience.

There are several other important aspects to Raynaud's disease. First of all, the effects are bilateral or symmetrical. Second, there is no identifiable medical aetiology. A number of causes have been mooted such as an overactive sympathetic nervous system rendering peripheral vessels more prone to constriction, a circulatory fault local to the affected extremities, and the possibility of high viscosity, i.e. thick, blood which would jeopardize free flow through the peripheral blood vessels. Whatever the precise cause, Raynaud's disease is a painful and worrying condition for those who suffer from it. The affected extremities are often scarred, cracked or ulcerated. It is also a persistent affliction, with the symptoms disappearing in warmer weather only to return with the cold of the following winter.

The traditional treatment for Raynaud's disease is to ensure that the susceptible extremities are kept warm and well-protected in cold weather. Drugs that stimulate vasodilation are prescribed occasionally and in some cases doctors have resorted to surgery of the sympathetic nervous system (sympathectomy). None of these treatments are completely satisfactory.

Consequently, a number of researchers have recently attempted to treat Raynaud's disease using biofeedback. Almost all of them have employed biofeedback of skin temperature. The voltage of a thermocouple and the electrical resistance of a thermistor vary systematically with changes in temperature, so either a thermocouple or a thermistor is attached to the affected extremity. The output from these devices can then be transformed to yield continuous feedback of skin temperature. Schwartz's (1972) study constitutes the exception. Here, biofeedback of peripheral vasodilation was used instead. A photoplethysmograph was applied to detect the vasomotor tone of the blood vessels in the affected area. This device consists of a minute light source and a photodetector cell, and the area of interest is placed between the two. The amount of light reaching the cell will vary with the amount of blood in the tissue between the light and the cell. As more blood equals less light, the detector cell indicates whether the peripheral vessels are constricted or dilated, and this information is transformed to provide a biofeedback facility.

Schwartz reported the application of biofeedback of peripheral vasodilation to two cases of Raynaud's disease. While the first patient received feedback of vasodilation from the toe, for the second patient, training focussed on increasing digital blood flow. Schwartz's account is essentially anecdotal and accordingly short of important detail, such as the extent and exact format of training. However, he relates that the first patient managed successfully to increase blood flow in the affected area and enjoyed complete relief of symptoms for a year-and-a-half when, with symptoms returning, further treatment was requested. In contrast, the second patient neither learned to control blood flow nor showed any clinical improvement.

Peper (1973) also presented an anecdotal case report. In this instance skin temperature biofeedback was used with a single patient. Few details are provided and although the patient evidently achieved some success in raising hand temperature, there was no remission of symptoms.

Surwit (1973) was somewhat more successful, at least in the short-term, using a combination of autogenic training and temperature biofeedback. In autogenic training, the individual is induced to relax by imagining, first that his hands and feet are heavy, and then that they are warm. Surwit's patient had endured Rayanud's disease for five years and had already undergone a sympathectomy. Although surgery had evidently relieved symptoms in the feet, the hands had remained susceptible. Biofeedback and autogenic training were continued for about a year, during which time the patient displayed an increase in hand temperature from 23 °C to 26.6 °C. The frequency of Raynaud's attacks was reported to have decreased markedly, but after treatment finished, the ability to influence temperature was lost, along with the clinical gains. Not surprisingly perhaps, the patient also displayed little interest in further biofeedback therapy.

Subsequent outcomes have been a little more encouraging. Jacobson et al. (1973) tried both hypnosis and temperature biofeedback in the treatment of a patient who had suffered Raynaud's disease for three years and whose symptoms were so severe that the patient feared amputation was the only recourse. Feedback was geared to producing increases in the temperature of the hand relative to that of the forehead. Treatment lasted for eight sessions. The first three sessions were given over to hypnosis, the patient being instructed to imagine scenes (e.g. a warm beach) likely to increase hand temperature. For the last five sessions, hypnosis was abandoned and temperature biofeedback provided instead. While no reliable increases in hand temperature occurred with hypnosis, temperature rose by about 4 °C during the biofeedback sessions. Control was reported to persist eventually in the absence of feedback, but no details were provided. The clinical effects were largely congruent. While only marginal improvements were evident during hypnosis, with biofeedback there was a marked reduction in the frequency of attacks. In addition, at follow-up some seven-and-a-half months after treatment, the patient indicated continued ability to influence hand temperature and a continued improvement in condition.

Blanchard and Haynes (1975) also employed biofeedback of hand-relative-to-forehead temperature to treat a patient with a long history of Raynaud's disease; cold hands and feet had been a problem for as long as she could remember. Following four sessions of baseline assessment, the patient received a total of twenty-four sessions of treatment arranged in four blocks of six sessions each. For the first and third blocks, the patient was instructed to increase hand temperature but no feedback was presented. In the second and final blocks of sessions, biofeedback was provided to aid efforts at hand-warming. Results indicated that during the feedback sessions, hand temperature rose on average by 3.4 °F. There were no reliable increases with instructions alone. By the end of the treatment period, hand temperature was some 12 °F higher than baseline. The patient also reported that the symptoms of Raynaud's disease had abated markedly. At seven-month follow-up, self-control of hand-warming was initially variable, but with five booster biofeedback sessions, control was quickly established. In addition, the patient continued to report clinical improvement.

Taub (1977) reported briefly on three patients given

temperature biofeedback to facilitate hand-warming. About twenty sessions of training were provided and all three patients learned to increase temperature by some 4° to 5 °F, with two of the three reporting fewer Raynaud's attacks during treatment. However, given the absence of procedural detail and systematic clinical data, independent evaluation of the effectiveness of treatment is extremely difficult.

Sunderman and Delk (1978) also furnished little in the way of formal outcome data, although they did provide a fuller description of procedure. A patient with a long history of Raynaud's disease was treated with temperature biofeedback for about thirteen months. Since the patient had discovered that silently quoting Biblical extracts increased hand temperature, a Bible was permitted to supplement the more typical apparatus in later sessions. Following rather inconsistent performances early in training, successful hand-warming was eventually achieved; the patient was usually able to increase hand temperature by more than 10 °F. Unfortunately, no systematic data on the incidence and severity of Raynaud's symptoms were presented, although Sunderman and Delk reported that the condition no longer disrupted the patient's life.

Only one paper to date has studied sufficient patients to compare biofeedback with another mode of treatment. Surwit et al. (1978) allocated thirty-two patients to one of four treatment conditions. Group 1 received autogenic training in the laboratory for six biweekly sessions and undertook additional practice at home. Group 2 attended the laboratory for the same number of sessions but were given temperature biofeedback in addition to autogenic training; they, too, practised autogenic exercise at home. Group 3 resembled group 1, but practised exclusively at home, attending the laboratory only for initial instructions, while group 4 was a home-based version of group 2. Overall, patients developed the ability to raise hand temperature, but there were no reliable group differences. Biofeedback in combination with autogenic training was no more effective than autogenic training alone, and those who practised exclusively at home did as well as those given laboratory training. A similar picture emerged with regard to Raynaud's disease. Overall, patients experienced a reduction in the frequency and severity of symptoms of up to 50 percent. While on average they suffered 2.3 attacks per day before treatment, with treatment the figure dropped to 1.6. Again, however, there were no group differences; biofeedback and autogenic training together afforded no more relief than autogenic training alone, and laboratory-based training added nothing of significance to home practice.

Until recently, the status of biofeedback in the treatment of Raynaud's disease rested on a series of case studies. A total of only ten patients had been studied and for many of these we are denied sufficient information to form an independent judgement. Of these ten patients, three apparently gained no relief at all, one improved but relapsed as soon as treatment ended, three showed some but possibly transitory benefits, and three showed reasonably sustained improvement. Given the problems inherent in case studies, this can hardly be regarded as a very compelling testament of efficacy. Finally in the one recent study which included large numbers, biofeedback was rather poorly indicated; it added nothing to the gains associated with a simpler alternative, autogenic training. Given that they are relatively inexpensive and easy to administer, autogenic exercises would seem a much better bet.

Chapter 4

Migraine

Introduction

Raynaud's disease is not the only condition to which temperature biofeedback has been applied. In fact, its most extensive use has been in the treatment of migraine and a substantial number of studies have now examined its efficacy in that context. This chapter will focus on that application.

Anyone who experiences migraine headaches can readily attest to their severity, but migraine is more than severe headache; it is frequently accompanied by feelings of nausea, vomiting may occur, and there may be an aversion to bright light. In addition, the headache is usually restricted to one side of the head. Faced with such symptoms, bed is often the only recourse and few migraine sufferers are able to cope with the usual business of the day once an attack has started. In many cases an attack is heralded by various prodromal symptoms which can include visual disturbances, sensory abnormalities elsewhere (such as numbness in a limb), speech and movement difficulties, changes in mood and appetite, constipation and water retention.

Although it is difficult to be precise, it would appear that as many as 5 per cent of the adult population suffer from migraine. Women seem to be more prone than men, although the reasons for this sex difference remain unclear.

While the causes and mechanisms of migraine are still something of a mystery, the blood vessels of the head and brain have been accorded a central role. Briefly, the prodromal effects are thought to reflect the constriction of these vessels to such an extent that brain blood flow is rendered inadequate and normal neurological functioning compromised. The subsequent headache is thought to stem from an overcompensatory, rebound vasodilation and as the arteries distend, so they encroach on pain receptors. In general, this account has received support from the study of both intracranial and extracranial blood vessels during and before headache. Finally, there is some, but yet rather equivocal, evidence to implicate both stress and diet as precipitating factors in migraine attacks.

Drugs that stimulate vasoconstriction have been prescribed in many instances. Unfortunately, they are not always effective and occasionally produce disruptive side effects. More recently, a group of compounds, beta-adrenergic blockers, designed to inhibit sympathetic nervous system activity have received attention, but as yet, migraine defies satisfactory chemical control.

Temperature biofeedback and migraine

The application of temperature biofeedback owes much to serendipity. Sargent et al. (1972) were exploring self-control of biological functions using a range of feedback facilities, including skin temperature biofeedback, when one of their subjects reported that she had recovered spontaneously from a migraine attack during the course of training. Her physiological responses were immediately examined and revealed a large and sudden increase of 10 °F in hand-relative-to-forehead temperature.

Inspired by this result, Sargent and his associates undertook a series of clinical trials using a combination of temperature biofeedback and autogenic training. At the start they favoured biofeedback of the temperature differential between the forehead and the index finger, and following initial training in the clinic, their patients practised raising digital-relative-to-forehead temperature daily with a portable feedback unit at home. As soon as they achieved success, the patients were encouraged to practise increasingly without the biofeedback facility. The full training course lasted about a year. For later patients, differential temperature feedback was abandoned, since with it, the precise basis of successful performance was difficult to determine, and feedback of absolute digital temperature was used instead.

Results have been presented in a series of reports (Sargent, Green and Walters, 1973; Sargent, Walters and Green, 1973; Solbach and Sargent 1977). In all, 110 migraine sufferers started the training programme, with 74 completing. Although few data are provided, the researchers consistently affirm that their patients were able to master temperature control. Clinical outcomes were presented in the form of global ratings of improvement. Five categories were applied; 'very good' (headaches had decreased in frequency and duration, and were at reduced severity; patient was able to recognise preheadache signals and prevent a headache; medication was effectively abandoned), 'good' (as above, save for the elimination of medication), 'moderate improvement' (reduced headache duration, frequency and severity; the patient was often able to abort headaches that had started, but was unable to avoid headaches and still reliant on medication), 'slight improvement' (some headache relief), and 'no improvement'. Of the 74 patients that lasted the course, 15 were rated as very good and 20 as good; 16 were considered to show moderate improvement, 11 slight improvement and 12 no improvement. Thus, combining the very good and good categories, we find that some 47 per cent of the total of 74 patients derived substantial clinical benefit. Solbach and Sargent's follow-up observations on 56 of the patients who completed the programme, as well as on 12 of the 'drop-outs', indicated that these clinical gains, both in terms of headache and medication, had largely been maintained. The drop-outs, as might be expected, exhibited less of a reduction in headache frequency than those who completed training.

While many researchers followed Sargent et al's lead, it must be pointed out that, although the original research was indeed promising, it could hardly be regarded as providing unequivocal evidence that biofeedback, alone or with autogenic training, represents a particularly effective treatment for migraine. As indicated, just about half of their patients demonstrated marked improvement, but methodological shortcomings mitigate all bar the most tentative of conclusions. In the absence of controls, the active component in the programme for those 50 per cent who benefited substantially cannot be established, nor is it possible to rule out the influence of placebo effects. In this context, it is worth noting that Sargent et al's patients reported that they found the autogenic relaxation exercises and staff interest and support to be the most useful parts of training. In addition, the rather subjective character of the clinical assessment procedure, which inevitably increases the risk of bias, and the general lack of quantitative data necessarily diminish the status of the research.

Further uncontrolled studies

The majority of subsequent studies of biofeedback and migraine have also fallen short in terms of methodological rigour. Accordingly, the evidence for biofeedback must be regarded with caution.

Wickramasekera (1973a) reported on two patients, treated first of all with electromyographic feedback from the frontalis muscles of the forehead for sixteen and eighteen weeks, followed by biofeedback of digital skin temperature for ten and eleven weeks respectively. During both phases of treatment, they were encouraged to practise at home. While no biological data are provided for the first phase, temperature feedback resulted in an elevation in hand temperature of more than 5 °F for both patients. With regard to clinical outcome, electromyographic feedback occasioned only marginal reductions in the incidence of headaches. Temperature biofeedback, however, was associated with a drop in headache frequency to around zero. These gains were still evident at three months follow-up.

Following five weeks of baseline assessment, Johnson and Turin (1975) exposed their single patient initially to twelve sessions of biofeedback for lowering hand temperature, with the misrepresentation that this had been found to be effective treatment for migraine. Twelve sessions of biofeedback for raising hand temperature were then given, and home practice was encouraged. Although the patient was able to reduce hand temperature by only 0.7 °F on average, an average increase of 2 °F was effected in the second series of sessions. Further, while headache activity increased from baseline during the twelve sessions of hand-cooling; a reduction in headache frequency occurred with hand-warming. Undoubtedly, this association between headache frequency and the direction of the temperature change, adds weight to the case for biofeedback. However, a general trend toward reduced headache activity during the baseline period makes interpretation of the decline with handwarming difficult. In addition, there was no follow-up evaluation.

Kentsmith et al. (1976) also applied hand-warming feedback to a single case. Treatment spanned several months and, in addition to biofeedback, various relaxation procedures including meditation were also used. Between sessions, the patient practised meditation and hand-warming with a portable instrument at home. Successful elevations in hand-warming were achieved and a 75 per cent decrease in the duration and intensity of headaches was reported. Although minimal details are given, the researchers stated that these gains were maintained at follow-up a year later.

Reading and Mohr (1976) treated six patients with

biofeedback for raising hand temperature. After baseline assessment, an unspecified number of biofeedback sessions were provided, followed by a single no-feedback session and two follow-up sessions, one month and two months later. Reading and Mohr's patients were able to increase hand temperature with feedback and maintained this ability in the final no-feedback session, where an average increase of 1.4 °C was recorded. Headache frequency was also reduced from 4.1 per week at baseline to 1.9 during treatment and 1.4 at the second follow-up. There was also a significant reduction in the average number of hours of headache from 25.3 hours per week during baseline to 10.4 during treatment and 5.1 at final follow-up.

Turin and Johnson (1976) provided data on seven patients, three of whom were given the same hand-cooling followed by hand-warming treatment as before. The other four received biofeedback for hand-warming throughout. Again, the hand-cooling feedback was only marginally successful at promoting reductions in hand temperature. However, all subjects were able to raise hand temperature, with average increases ranging from 0.1 °C to 1.7 °C. Further, while no improvement in headache activity was evident with attempted hand-cooling, all subjects showed at least some improvement with hand-warming: during the final weeks of training, headache incidence had dropped to 1.3 per week from 2.2 per week before treatment and the average number of hours with headaches had dropped from 12.4 hours per week to 5.7 in the same period. Again, however, there was no follow-up assessment to establish the durability of these gains.

In a study which included patients with other than migraine headaches, Fried et al. (1977) reported on three unambiguous migraine sufferers. Patients received both electromyographic and temperature biofeedback in the laboratory and were given portable temperature units for home practice, with taped instructions regarding autogenic relaxation. No physiological data are furnished, but the clinical results indicate that one of the migraine patients showed a 75 per cent reduction in headache frequency and severity. Unfortunately, the other two displayed little improvement. Again, there was no follow-up, so that even their single success might have relapsed with time.

Studies with larger samples

A number of reports have presented results on much larger samples of patients. Of the 58 patients treated by Adler and Adler (1976), for example, 22 were migraine sufferers. Following initial exposure to electromyographic biofeedback temperature biofeedback was introduced as the main treatment facility. Unfortunately, only the scantiest of data were reported; at follow-up, though, 81 per cent of the migraine patients apparently displayed a 75 per cent or greater reduction in headache frequency. However, it is difficult to attach much weight to this result in the absence of so much important information.

Medina et al. (1976) were more generous with detail. Of the twenty-seven patients treated, thirteen had migraine headaches. Treatment was undertaken twice weekly for four weeks and in each session, training with both frontalis electromyographic and temperature biofeedback was provided. In addition, a portable temperature feedback unit was leased for home practice and booster sessions were held in the laboratory once every two months. Hand-warming was accomplished successfully and five of the migraine patients showed at least a 50 per cent improvement in the frequency and severity of headaches. Another four showed improvement in the 30–50 per cent range. At follow-up between six and thirty-three months, apparently these gains were maintained.

Mitch et al. (1976) included twelve migraine patients in a total sample of twenty headache sufferers. The other eight were mixed migraine and tension headache patients. Treatment began in the laboratory; autogenic relaxation instructions were given in combination with biofeedback for hand-warming. However, laboratory-based treatment was quickly superseded by home-based practice; a portable temperature feedback unit was provided and patients were encouraged to practise if they felt a headache coming on. Data for all twenty patients were reported together, although the migraine patients evidently responded better than the mixed patients. All bar one patient managed to increase hand temperature successfully, and 65 per cent improved on two or more of the clinical criteria (headache intensity, frequency, duration and medication use). These gains were maintained in the patients sampled at follow-up six months later.

Although these three studies commendably have included fairly large samples of patients, they are no more sophisticated in terms of experimental design than the more modest endeavours discussed earlier. They still lack the control conditions necessary to establish temperature biofeedback unambiguously as an effective treatment for migraine. While all three reported sustained improvements in a respectable proportion of their patients, they all used complex treatment packages, of which temperature biofeedback was but one element. The influence of the other elements, autogenic relaxation, electromyographic biofeedback, as well as the possible placebos of attention, a novel treatment and impressive instrumentation, must be discounted satisfactorily before biofeedback can be established as the key element.

Controlled studies

Only a few studies have attempted the sort of experimental control necessary to assess efficacy properly. The earliest was reported by Andreychuk and Skriver (1975). Twenty-eight migraine patients were assigned to one of three groups. Group 1 received training with temperature biofeedback plus autogenic relaxation instruction. Group 2 was given biofeedback of the alpha waves from their brain wave (electroencephalograph) records combined with relaxation instructions. The final group was treated with autohypnosis which consisted of relaxation instructions, visual imagery and direct suggestions for dealing with pain. Patients in all three groups received ten weekly sessions and were encouraged to practise at home between sessions. Clinical outcome was assessed in terms of a self-rating headache index, defined as the product of the number of headache hours and the severity of the headaches experienced. On average, group 1 achieved a 75 per cent improvement, while group 2 and 3 averaged 43 per cent and 36 per cent improvement respectively; these differences, however, were not statistically significant. In addition, regardless of treatment groups, patients high in hypnotic susceptibility improved significantly more than patients low in susceptibility. The respective average improvement rates were 71 per cent and 41 per cent.

These results hardly afford conclusive evidence for temperature biofeedback in the treatment of migraine. While the temperature feedback group recorded the highest average rate of improvement, the absence of statistically reliable differences among groups mitigates all bar the most tentative of interpretations. The absence of a follow-up places a further qualification on any conclusion of efficacy.

In a more recent study, Blanchard et al. (1978) allocated thirty migraine sufferers to one of three equally-sized treatment groups. Group 1 received temperature biofeedback plus autogenic training; group 2 was given training in progressive relaxation; group 3 was a waiting list (no treatment) control group. The two active treatment groups attended for twelve biweekly sessions. Patients in both the biofeedback and relaxation groups showed significantly greater reductions in headache frequency and intensity than the waiting list control patients. However, there were no reliable differences between the biofeedback and relaxation groups. At one month follow-up, by which time some of the waiting list control patients had been treated and added to the analysis, nine out of the thirteen now in group 1 and all twelve out of the twelve available in group 2 displayed improvement (where improvement was defined as a reduction in headache frequency and/or intensity) greater than 25 per cent. These group outcome rates were not reliably different. At three month follow-up, the respective rates of improvement for the biofeedback and progressive relaxation groups were seven out of ten patients and seven out of nine patients. Thus, although temperature biofeedback plus autogenic instructions would seem to effect reasonable relief from migraine, the combination is no more effective than progressive relaxation, a simpler, less expensive, and more easily applied alternative. Silver et al. (1979) reported on a one year follow-up of eighteen of these patients. Improvements were maintained, but there were still no group differences to speak of.

True temperature feedback was compared with false temperature feedback in a study by Mullinix et al. (1978), in an attempt to allow for the likely placebo effects of biofeedback therapy. Twelve migraine patients were allocated to one of two groups. While one group received veridical feedback of digital temperature, the other was given false temperature information. In all other respects, however, the instruction and treatment given were identical for the two groups. Nine sessions of treatment were spread over an eight to nine week period. While exact data were not presented, Mullinix et al. affirmed that the veridical feedback group displayed a significantly greater overall average increase in digital temperature than the false feedback group. However, there was no analogous difference in clinical outcome. While four of the six true feedback patients showed at least some improvement in self-reported headache activity following treatment, so did three of the five false feedback patients (one was eliminated because of incomplete self-report).

Finally, Kewman and Roberts (1980) compared biofeedback for hand-warming with biofeedback for hand-cooling in an admirably sophisticated experiment. A double-blind design was employed, whereby neither patient nor experimenter knew the direction of the required temperature response. In all, three groups of patients were studied. Group 1 comprised eleven patients given feedback for hand-warming; group 2 comprised twelve patients given feedback for hand-cooling; group 3 comprised eleven patients who attended the laboratory for the same amount of time but were subject to no specific treatment. The study consisted of six weeks of baseline assessment, followed by ten weekly laboratory sessions, and finally six weeks of post treatment assessment. While the biofeedback training effected differences in hand temperature between groups 1 and 2, no parallel differences in headache duration and frequency were evident, a result somewhat at odds with Turin and Johnson's findings. In addition, improvement rates for patients trained in hand-warming were not demonstrably better than those recorded for the no-treatment control patients.

Biofeedback for forehead blood flow

Biofeedback of temporal artery pulse amplitude to encourage forehead vasoconstriction, has been advocated as an alternative to feedback for hand-warming or digital vasodilation. However, as yet only three published studies have explored this alternative using anything approaching a sensitive experimental design.

Friar and Beatty (1976) assigned nineteen patients with histories of migraine to one of two groups. The first group of ten patients received eight sessions of feedback of temporal artery pulse amplitude, and were trained to increase forehead vasoconstriction. The remaining nine patients were given analogous training, but in reducing digital pulse amplitude, the vascular response opposite to that sought with hand-warming biofeedback. Patients in both groups were able to achieve vasoconstriction at the appropriate site. In addition, the group given biofeedback of forehead blood flow improved significantly more than the digital feedback group in terms of headache activity. While the former reported a 36 per cent decrease in headache frequency, the latter recorded only a 14 per cent reduction. Although these results are encouraging, it is a pity that Friar and Beatty did not include a more telling comparison group, such as one given relaxation training or provided with biofeedback for digital vasodilation. This would have permitted a much more rigorous test of the forehead feedback alternative.

Bild and Adams' (1980) study is open to similar criticism. Following six weeks of baseline assessment, three groups were formed. Group 1 comprised seven migraine patients who subsequently attended for ten sessions of biofeedback of temporal artery pulse amplitude; there were two to three sessions weekly. Group 2 had six patients, who received training for a similar duration, but with frontalis EMG feedback. The six patients in group 3 constituted a no-treatment control. Both of the active treatment groups mastered biological control and both demonstrated significant improvements in headache activity following treatment. By six weeks follow-up, headache frequency had dropped from a baseline level of 2.7 headaches per week to 1.0 per week for the pulse amplitude feedback group, and from 2.2 to 1.4 per week for the EMG feedback group. The no-treatment group derived no such benefit, with headache frequency figures of 2.4 and 2.0 respectively. With regard to headache duration, the pulse amplitude group showed a decrease from 29.4 to 7.5 hours per week, and the EMG group a decrease from 24.4 to 10.4. Again the no-treatment group demonstrated no changes; the figures this time were 18.9 at baseline and 19.9 at follow-up. While the pulse amplitude patients would appear to have benefited most, differences between them and the EMG biofeedback patients were not statistically reliable. The pulse amplitude patients were assessed again, three months later and demonstrated continuing improvements; average headache frequency was 0.8 per weekend and average headache duration 5.7 hours per week. It is unfortunate, though, that Bild and Adams did not subject the EMG group to the same protracted scrutiny.

Cohen et al. (1980) recently undertook the sort of comparison necessary to establish the relative efficacy of temporal artery biofeedback. Four treatments were compared in a study which initially included 42 migraine sufferers. Following eight weeks of baseline evaluation, 10 of these patients received biofeedback of temporal artery pulse amplitude, 11 received biofeedback of differential digital-forehead temperature, 11 were given frontalis EMG feedback, and 10 received biofeedback to facilitate the enhancement of brain wave alpha rhythm. Treatment continued for between eight and ten weeks and in all comprised twenty-four training sessions. Patients were subsequently monitored for up to eight months after treatment, although only thirty-four patients (8 in the temperative feedback group, 8 in the pulse amplitude group, 9 in the EMG group and 9 in the alpha group) completed follow-up evaluation. Overall, Cohen et al.'s patients displayed a reduction from baseline to eight week post-treatment of about 20 per cent in the average number of headaches experienced each week. This improvement was still evident at eight months. However, the different biofeedback groups showed roughly equivalent levels of improvement, i.e., no one feedback modality was more effective than another.

Conclusions

While a fair number of migraine patients would now appear to have gained benefit or relief from the application of temperature biofeedback, lingering doubts must remain. These improvements have almost invariably emerged in uncontrolled studies, in which patients have often been exposed to quite complex treatment packages, which include, in addition to temperature feedback, training or instructions regarding relaxation, the manipulation of imagery, and feedback of other functions, notably muscle tension. Further, the few studies which have incorporated control conditions paint a rather discouraging picture. Although temperature biofeedback still proves effective, i.e. improvements are still registered either relative to pretreatment or to no treatment, it is no more effective than the more easily and economically applied alternative of relaxation training. Finally, the results of the one study which deployed a false feedback control strongly imply that much of the impact of hand-warming biofeedback is non-specific and that, in fact, the treatment constitutes little more than a rather elaborate placebo. While feedback of forehead blood flow might prove a more effective facility, it has, as yet, received little formal experimental attention and its relative efficacy has still to be established. The recent results of Cohen et al. (1980), however, are not very encouraging.

Chapter 5

Tension headaches

Introduction

Decidedly more common than vascular or migraine headaches are muscular or tension headaches. Surveys (e.g. Waters 1970; 1974) indicate that the latter are some three or four times more prevalent. While they are rarely incapacitating in the same way as migraine attacks, they nonetheless often involve severe pain and in some individuals occur with alarming frequency.

As Olton and Noonberg (1980) pointed out, the term 'tension' signifies three aspects of such headaches. First, it refers to the subjectively experienced symptoms described typically as a 'tightness' or 'pressure' usually of the forehead, but sometimes located at the back of the head and neck. As indicated, tension headaches, although severe, are seldom as debilitating as migraines, and are rarely associated with the nausea that commonly characterizes a migraine attack. Further, with tension headaches, prodromal symptoms are generally absent, and the pain is frequently bilateral, while in migraine it is usually confined to one side of the head (Friedman et al. 1954).

Secondly, the word tension denotes the contracted state of the head muscles involved, usually the forehead frontalis muscles. Measurements of frontalis muscle activity in headache sufferers, in the absence or presence of a tension headache, reveal striking differences in the extent of muscle tension; decidedly greater tension is recorded during the occurrence of a headache (e.g. Budzynski et al 1973; Sainsbury and Gibson 1954; Tunis and Wolff 1954). Further, comparisons of muscle tension between headache sufferers and non-sufferers attest to much higher residual tension levels for the former, particularly in the forehead frontalis muscles (e.g. Budzynski, et al 1973; Haynes et al. 1975; Philips, 1978).

Finally, the term 'tension' characterizes the social circumstances and emotional milieu associated with the occurrence of such headaches. There is a fair deal of evidence to implicate psychological stress as a precipitating and sustaining factor (see Rachman and Philips 1978).

Given the role of forehead muscle contraction in tension headaches, the reduction of frontalis muscle tension would seem a sensible therapeutic objective. Unfortunately, the frontalis muscle may be particularly difficult to relax. As Rachman and Philips (1978) have pointed out, even when patients are able to relax their general musculature quite adequately their frontalis muscles often still display noticeable tension. Such intransigence clearly suggests the need for external assistance; biofeedback seemed an obvious candidate.

Muscle tension measurement and biofeedback

It has been appreciated for well over a century that tension in skeletal muscles is associated with measureable electrical activity, usually referred to as electromyographic (EMG) activity. With the use of a pair of small metal electrodes applied to the surface of the skin above a particular muscle, such as the forehead frontalis muscle, and appropriate electronic amplification, the tension in the muscle can be recorded as a characteristically spiky trace. EMG activity increases as muscle contraction increases, i.e. the amplitude of the recorded spikes will vary directly with the extent of the muscle tension. A muscle consists of millions of separate muscle fibres bound together by connective tissue, and it is the collected electrical discharges of the fibres, which precipitate mechanical contraction, that are reflected in an EMG trace.

Unfortunately, the raw EMG trace is rather capricious and difficult to interpret as feedback. Consequently, it is usual to transform the trace either by selecting the largest electrical discharge occurring in a given period of time, say a second, or by counting the total number of spikes which exceed a particular criterion during the specified time period. The transformed or integrated EMG signal is then exploited for the purposes of feedback. Feedback can be either binary or analogue, visual or auditory.

The efficacy of EMG biofeedback: uncontrolled studies

The first study to apply EMG biofeedback in the treatment of tension headaches was reported by Budzynski et al. (1970). Five patients were exposed to a variable number of sessions over a period of four to eight weeks. During the first two sessions, the patients were encouraged to relax, but without the aid of feedback. Frontalis EMG feedback was provided in subsequent sessions, and as training progressed, so the criterion for feedback changed, i.e. patients had to achieve progressively greater decreases in forehead EMG activity in order to receive the same biofeedback signal indicating reductions in muscle tension. In addition, patients were told to practise relaxing their frontalis muscles at home, and trials without feedback were introduced into later laboratory sessions.

All five patients managed to decrease frontalis EMG during the course of training. EMG levels dropped on average from 5.8 microvolts before feedback training to 3.5 microvolts by the end of the fourth week. In addition, headache activity also decreased. The average hourly headache activity, subjectively rated between zero and five, decreased from a pre-training value of 0.84 to 0.30 after the fourth week of training. At three-month follow-up these clinical gains were largely maintained. In three of the five patients, headaches had ceased virtually altogether, while for the other two they were reported to persist, but at much reduced levels.

Again, this study is subject to the criticisms levelled at uncontrolled studies in previous chapters. Nevertheless, the indications of therapeutic efficacy were certainly sufficient to warrant further study, and several researchers rightly responded to Budzynski et al's lead.

Wickramasekera (1973b) subsequently reported on five patients with protracted histories of almost daily tension headaches. Following the initial assessment of baseline frontalis EMG activity, patients practised relaxation at three consecutive daily sessions, and were then provided with frontalis EMG biofeedback for a further nine sessions, spread over three weeks. While EMG activity changed little during relaxation, with EMG biofeedback sustained decreases were observed; on average EMG levels dropped from 14 microvolts at baseline assessment to around 5 microvolts during feedback. This decrease was still evident at follow-up nine weeks later. Parallel findings were obtained with regard to headache activity. While the average rating of headache intensity was 4.5 at baseline and only the most marginal reduction was recorded with relaxation, the averaged rating following EMG biofeedback was 1.9. By follow-up, the average headache intensity rating had fallen even further to 0.5. These results are encouraging, but again given the uncontrolled nature of the study, a certain amount of caution is warranted. While Wickramasekera did attempt some sort of comparison between EMG biofeedback and relaxation procedures, it is hardly satisfactory; differences in both the order and the extent of the treatments undoubtedly favour biofeedback.

Epstein et al. (1974) treated a single patient whose headaches were so severe that he had to be hospitalized. Following six sessions of baseline measurement, the patient received six sessions of frontalis EMG biofeedback. A further six baseline sessions were then undertaken, followed once again by six sessions of biofeedback.

On release from hospital, the patient attended as an out-patient for a second course of treatment comprising four sessions, each of which consisted of a baseline period followed by exposure to EMG biofeedback and, finally, by a series of no-feedback trials for which the patient was instructed simply to relax as much as possible.

During the first course of treatment, frontalis EMG activity dropped considerably with the provision of feed-back; the average level during the two baseline periods was 39 and 30 microvolts respectively, compared to 23 and 15 microvolts during the two feedback phases. Unfortunately, this reduction was not maintained following release from hospital. However, when feedback was reinstated during the second course of treatment, frontalis EMG activity again decreased, only to rise again during the no-feedback trials. Clearly, for this patient, significant reductions in forehead muscle tension were evident only during the presence of the feedback facility; there was no evidence of generalization. The headache data told a similar story. Headache intensity was rated at 5.0 and 5.8 during the two initial baseline periods, whereas it was rated as 3.5 and 2.5 during the two feedback phases. However, by the start of the second course of treatment, headache intensity had arisen once more to 6.2 and, although it decreased to 4.8 with further EMG feedback, six days after the second course of treatment it had risen to the even higher level of 10.8 More powerful medication was then prescribed and the subject received training in yoga. At seven-month follow-up, the patient reported some relief, but no formal data were provided. In any event given previous indications, this improvement could hardly be attributed to biofeedback.

Reeves (1976) presented a decidely more optimistic single-case report. Treatment was arranged in three phases, with phase 1 being used for baseline measurement. In addition to monitoring frontalis EMG and headache activity, Reeves required the patient to record the circumstances in which headaches occurred. Phase 2 comprised six sessions of cognitive skills training. Here the patient was counselled on how to cope more positively with pertinent environmental stressors. Phase 3 comprised eighteen sessions of frontalis EMG feedback. While no decreases in EMG level were observed during phase 2, EMG dropped from 9 to about 5 microvolts during the feedback phase. Headache activity also abated with treatment. Whereas the average hourly headache activity (defined as a product of duration and severity) was 1.9 at baseline, it fell to 1.2 following cognitive skills training, and to 0.6 with biofeedback. At follow-up, six months later, these gains were still evident; EMG level remained around 5 microvolts and headache activity attracted a score of 0.5.

Wickramasekera's (1976) single patient fared less well. Given EMG feedback for a total of eighteen training sessions and encouraged to practise twice daily at home, the patient eventually displayed an ability to reduce EMG levels rapidly. By the seventeenth session, reductions to less than 3 microvolts were achieved from a high baseline. Further, by later sessions a noticeable decline in headache activity was reported. However, the gains were not maintained, and at eight month follow-up, the patients's headaches were once again very prevalent.

Epstein and Abel (1977) treated six patients and their results seem to strengthen the general impression given by the case studies considered so far; that EMG biofeedback works for some individuals but not for others. Sixteen sessions of treatment were provided, each consisting of 10 minutes baseline EMG monitoring, 20 minutes of frontalis EMG biofeedback, and a final 20 minute period during which patients attempted to relax in the absence of biofeedback but using the techniques developed during the feedback phase. EMG levels declined with biofeedback, and although the overall shift was slight, from 19.4 microvolts at baseline to 17.8 microvolts during feedback, five out of the six patients managed consistent decreases. In the non-feedback phase, however, none of the six displayed reliable reductions in EMG activity. Headache activity was measured as a product of rated duration and rated severity. A far from uniform picture emerged; three of the patient showed a greater than 50 per cent improvement, two showed only the most marginal change, and one got slightly worse. The same spread of outcomes was recorded at follow-up up to eighteen months later.

In a study of fairly large numbers of headache sufferers, Peck and Kraft (1977) also reported a range of outcomes, although their overall results were more encouraging than those of Epstein and Abel. EMG biofeedback from either the forehead or the neck was provided for a minimum of seven sessions; the average number of sessions was eleven. EMG activity decreased with feedback by some 30 per cent on average. Headache activity, measured in much the same way as in the Epstein and Abel study, showed a parallel reduction. The overall average decrease in headache activity was 50 per cent, with six of the patients reporting reductions in the 66–100 per cent range, six registering some benefit, (reductions in the 33–65 per cent range) and three showing little change, (reductions in headache activity less than 33 per cent). At follow-up, seven weeks after treatment, some relapse was evident, but average headache activity was still 40 per cent lower than at pretreatment assessment: a statistically reliable reduction.

As emphasized earlier, the results from uncontrolled studies of this sort can never establish fully the efficacy of a treatment. While they can offer useful pointers to effectiveness as they would seem to do in this instance, rigorously controlled experiments are necessary before explanations in terms of placebo and simple improvement with time can be discounted.

Studies attempting placebo control

Budzynski et al. (1973) were among the first to attempt placebo control in this context. Eighteen headache sufferers were assigned to one of three groups. Group 1 were given auditory EMG feedback from the frontalis site for a total of sixteen sessions. They were also encouraged to practise at home the strategies that effectively reduced muscle tension in the laboratory. Group 2 were given false EMG feedback. However, anticipating that their patients might guess the bogus nature of the feedback, Budzynski et al. engaged in further deception and represented the feedback 'clicks', not as EMG-derived, but as unrelated aids to relaxation, that would counter distracting and arousing thoughts. Again, sixteen sessions of treatment were provided. The third group received no treatment whatsoever.

Only group 1 showed a reliable decrease in EMG activity, and, as measured by the duration-mulitiplied-by-severity index already mentioned, they were the only group to report significant symptom relief. Four out of the six subjects in group 1 showed a greater than 66 per cent reduction in headache activity. These gains were still evident three and eighteen months after treatment. While these data certainly add to the case for biofeedback in the treatment of tension headaches, some qualifications are in order. First of all, the groups differed in respects other than the presence or veracity of feedback; group 1 patients were required to practise regularly at home what they had learned in the laboratory. No such demand for home relaxation was made of group 2 patients. Secondly, given that Budzynski et al. represented the bogus feedback as independent of EMG activity, it is questionable whether this condition offered adequate placebo control. In addition, the rationale actually provided may have been less than credible. The high, group 2 drop-out rate (four out of six patients abandoned treatment) inevitably reinforces these suspicions.

Philips's (1977) placebo control condition is subject to the same criticisms. Fifteen tension headache and mixed tension-migraine patients were assigned to one of two treatment conditions. Save for the home practice requirement, the two conditions were identical to those experienced by Budzynski et al.'s first two groups. Veridical and false feedback were provided for a total of twelve sessions, and EMG levels decreased substantially only for the patients given veridical feedback. In addition, this group reported an average reduction in headache frequency of approximately 30 per cent, while the bogus feedback patients improved by only 16 per cent on average. However, this difference was not statistically reliable. Nevertheless, the veridical feedback patients demonstrated further post treatment improvement, and at follow-up, six to eight weeks after treatment, differed significantly from the false feedback patients in terms of reported headache intensity, although not with regard to frequency.

In contrast to the last two studies, Wickramasekera (1972a) actually told his patients that the false feedback provision reflected true EMG levels and their subsequent comments indicated that they did not suspect the deception. Following a three-week period of baseline observation, five headache sufferers were given six sessions of bogus EMG feedback, followed by six sessions of veridical feedback. While EMG levels did not change appreciably with the introduction of false feedback, they decreased by more than 50 per cent during true feedback. Headache intensity (rate from 0 to 5) and frequency were similarly affected. Although neither changed with false feedback, frequency dropped from fifteen hours per week at baseline to four hours per week during the verdicial feedback phase and intensity decreased from 4 to 1.7. These gains were maintained at follow-up, nine weeks after treatment.

Kondo and Canter (1977) also provided false feedback with the assurance that it represented actual EMG activity. Following a fairly extensive (ten days) baseline assessment, twenty tension and mixed tension-migraine headache patients were allocated to one of two groups. The ten patients in group 1 received ten sessions of true frontalis EMG biofeedback; in contrast, group 2 patients were given ten sessions of false feedback. While group 2 patients showed little change in EMG activity, patients in group 1 demonstrated a substantial reduction with tension levels by the end of feedback some 50 per cent down relative to baseline values. A similar pattern of results was obtained for headache frequency. By the later sessions of true feedback, headache frequency had dropped from 5.2 per day at baseline to 1.0 per day. On the other hand, the false feedback patients reported only the most marginal change: from 4.5 per day to 3.5 per day. These group differences in improvement were statistically reliable. In addition, the differences held up at follow-up, twelve months after treatment. While the condition of the false feedback patients remained no different, four of the five veridical feedback patients contacted indicated that headache frequency had stayed low.

These last two studies provide a forceful counter to the objection that EMG biofeedback is little more than a rather elaborate placebo. Since their placebo control conditions mirrored the biofeedback treatment in every way, save for the veracity of the feedback, but occasioned nothing of the clinical benefit gained from true feedback, a specific therapeutic influence would seem to have been exerted by the biofeedback facility in these studies.

Cram (1980) also conducted a study which bears on the placebo issue. Following a three-week period of baseline assessment, thirty-two chronic headache sufferers were randomly assigned to one of four treatment groups. Group 1 were given auditory EMG feedback to facilitate reductions in frontalis muscle tension; group 2 also received EMG feedback but were instructed to use the facility to stabilize frontalis tension at baseline levels; group 3 received false EMG feedback, with instructions to use the feedback tone as a focus for meditation; group 4 were a no-treatment control. Treatment lasted three weeks, with two sessions per week. Only group 1 displayed a significant reduction in EMG with treatment; group 2 registered significantly higher EMG levels than group 3, who in turn showed significantly higher levels than group 1. With regard to headache activity, a somewhat different picture emerged. Patients in both groups 1 and 2 reported reliable reductions in headache activity; patients in the other two groups reported little or no change. At follow-up six months after treatment, group 1 patients showed something of a relapse, while for group 2 in contrast, treatment gains were maintained. While this study strongly implicates EMG biofeedback in headache amelioration, it also raises questions about the exact mechanisms involved. Clearly, it strongly suggests that muscle tension reduction is not a necessary element.

The results of a recent study by Carrobles et al. (1981) also suggest that EMG biofeedback can provide benefit over and above the effects ensuing from expectancy of relief. At the same time, however, their data bear testament to the healing power of expectancy *per se*. Following two weeks of baseline evaluation, nine patients were allocated to one of two groups. The first group of five patients were provided with frontalis EMG biofeedback for a total of eight sessions spread over four weeks. The four patients in the second group were given a high expectation of cure by informing them that their condition was temporary and relief inevitable; frontalis EMG was measured but no feedback provided. Immediate post treatment evaluation revealed that while reported headache frequency had dropped only marginally from 7.0 to 5.2 headache hours per day for this expectation group, a dramatic reduction, from 7.5 to 1.0 was registered for the biofeedback group. This latter improvement was still evident at follow-up, ten months later. It is important to note, though, that forty patients actually started this study. Eight were abandoned for mainly administrative and personal reasons; however, the remaining twenty-three improved to such an extent during baseline assessment to mitigate further treatment. Required simply to chart headache activity regularly, and subjected only to EMG measurement without feedback, average headache frequency dropped from 7.0 hours per day during the first week to 1.0 hour per day during the second week of baseline.

Studies comparing EMG biofeedback with other treatments

While EMG biofeedback indeed seems to afford some sort of direct benefit, the question remains as to whether it affords greater benefit than other, possibly more cost-effective alternatives. Cox et al. (1975) assigned twenty-seven tension headache sufferers to one of three treatment conditions. Group 1 was given eight sessions of frontalis EMG biofeedback along with a type of relaxation training which focussed on breathing and breath control. Group 2 also received this type of relaxation training for eight sessions, coupled this time with progressive relaxation training (as previously described). Group 3 were administered placebo medication; pharmacologically inactive capsules were dispensed at weekly intervals. EMG measures taken before and after treatment indicated that tension levels had dropped for the first two groups, but not for the final group. Headache activity was affected in a parallel fashion. While groups 1 and 2 showed a much greater reduction in headache activity (severity and duration) than group 3, they did not differ reliably from each other in this regard: the reductions in headache activity were 62, 53 and 19 per cent for groups 1, 2 and 3 respectively. The picture was much the same at follow-up one month later. Unfortunately, interpretation is difficult because the two treatments for comparison, EMG biofeedback and progressive relaxation training, are both confounded with a third treatment.

No such difficulties attend the study conducted by Haynes et al. (1975). Again, there were three treatment groups, each consisting this time of seven headache patients. Group 1 were provided with frontalis EMG feedback, group 2 with formal guidance regarding passive relaxation, while group 3 were asked simply to sit still and relax. Each group received six sessions of its designated treatment. A headache index was computed from self-reported headache frequency and intensity. Group 1 registered an 82 per cent reduction in this index with treatment, group 2 a 75 per cent reduction and group 3 only a 28 per cent reduction. Groups 1 and 2 were not reliably different. Follow-up evaluations, five to seven months after treatment, confirmed the impression that EMG biofeedback was no more effective than an easily administered set of relaxation instructions.

Chesney and Shelton (1976) also reported that biofeedback offered no advantage over a simple relaxation procedure; if anything, the relaxation training seemed the more effective treatment. Twenty-four headache sufferers were divided into four groups. Group 1 received EMG biofeedback, group 2 relaxation training, group 3 biofeedback plus relaxation, while group 4 was a no-treatment control. For both headache frequency and intensity the same pattern of results emerged. Groups 2 and 3 made impressive gains with treatment and improved more than groups 1 and 4. However, without frontalis EMG data and follow-up evaluation, only the most tentative conclusions can be drawn regarding relative efficacy from this study.

Hutchings and Reinking (1976) compared EMG biofeedback with a combination of autogenic and progressive relaxation procedures. Eighteen headache sufferers were exposed to one of three treatment regimes. Group 1 was provided with frontalis EMG feedback; group 2 was treated with a relaxation scheme which, as indicated, included elements of both autogenic and progressive relaxation training; group 3 received EMG feedback plus relaxation training. Treatment for all modes was continued for ten sessions. Group 1 and 3 displayed the largest reductions in frontalis EMG activity. Tension levels from these groups decreased by more than 66 per cent, compared to a drop of approximately 50 per cent for group 2. The biofeedback groups also registered a more substantial reduction in headache activity (defined as the product of the number of headache hours and the intensity of the headaches suffered). While group 2 patients reported only fairly minimal benefit, those in groups 1 and 3 reported 50 per cent and 70 per cent reductions in headache activity respectively. A short-term follow-up evaluation, twenty-nine days after treatment, confirmed these differential rates of improvement. While these data clearly favour biofeedback over relaxation, caution is warranted. With longer-term follow-up (see Reinking and Hutchings 1981) the early advantages of biofeedback were apparently lost and biofeedback and relaxation produced largely equivalent improvement rates.

Martin and Mathews (1978) also compared EMG biofeedback, either from the neck or the forehead musculature with progressive relaxation training. Twenty-four patients were assigned in equal numbers to either the feedback or the relaxation condition. Treatment comprised fourteen weekly sessions, and follow-up assessments were undertaken at one month and three months. While headache activity declined over treatment session for both groups, no group differences emerged either during or following treatment.

Finally, in a recent study Hart and Cichanski (1981) compared biofeedback directly from forehead and neck muscle sites. Two groups of ten tension headache patients attended between seven and fifteen weekly biofeedback sessions. The ten neck feedback patients received an average of 12.8 training sessions and the forehead patients an average of 13.0 sessions. While pre and post treatment comparisons revealed significant overall improvement, no group differences were apparent. With biofeedback from the neck, headache activity dropped from an initial average level of 1.48 to 0.63 following treatment; with biofeedback from the forehead, the corresponding figures were 1.57 and 0.86.

Concluding remarks

While the balance of data from uncontrolled investigations commends frontalis EMG feedback as an effective intervention for tension headaches, controlled experiments will always be necessary to establish a therapy unequivocally. In contrast to other areas of application, a number of studies deploying false feedback to control for possible nonspecific effects have now been carried out. Their results strongly suggest that the effect of EMG biofeedback cannot be discounted simply as artifacts of impressive gadgetry and the expectancy of relief. However, the observations of Carrobles et al. (1981) should act as sharp reminders of the healing power of expectancy in this context. Further, the precise mechanisms of biofeedback's influence remain unclear. Cram's (1980) results certainly challenge the assumption that it is the muscle tension reduction facilitated by feedback that is crucial, since feedback-assisted stablilization of EMG at high levels proved equally effective in alleviating headaches. Finally, it still remains to be demonstrated that biofeedback is more effective than simpler and less technologically elaborate alternatives. The evidence here is not very encouraging. EMG biofeedback generally emerges as no more effective than relatively simple relaxation procedures. There is one exception to this general result (Hutchings and Reinking 1976), but even in this case, the advantage of biofeedback over relaxation appeared to be short-lived.

Chapter 6

Neuromuscular Dysfunctions

Introduction

EMG biofeedback has also been widely applied to neuromuscular rehabilitation in an attempt to establish or recover normal functioning in muscles that behave abnormally. In some instances the aim is to restore activity to paralysed muscles, while in others it is the opposite, i.e. to curb excessive or inappropriate muscle activity. A wide range of specific dysfunctions have now received attention, with the most popular therapeutic foci being hemiplegia, peripheral nerve damage, spasmodic torticollis and cerebral palsy.

Hemiplegia

Hemiplegia refers to paralysis on one side of the body, typically as a result of a stroke. The particular side of dysfunction depends on the hemisphere of the vascular accident, and the scope of the paralysis depends on the extent and location of the cerebral damage. Traditionally, treatment has consisted of physical therapy and exercise, but improvement is far from assured.

The underlying rationale for biofeedback in cases of hemiplegia is that there exists some residual functioning in the affected muscles, which although insufficient to cause visible movement, is sufficient for EMG measurement and feedback. This, albeit minimal, electrical activity can then be built up and elaborated via the feedback facility until discernible movement is achieved. As movement becomes visible, visual feedback from the movement *per se* can supplement and eventually take over from the EMG feedback. Because of the minimal nature of functioning at the start of treatment, needle electrodes inserted into the relevant muscles are used instead of the surface electrodes employed with tension headache patients.

In an early study Andrews (1964) provided twenty hemiplegic patients with EMG feedback from needle electrodes located in the biceps and triceps muscles. Following electrode insertion, the muscles were manually manipulated through their usual range of motion. With the aid of visual EMG feedback, patients then attempted to generate EMG activity. Andrews reported that within five minutes, seventeen of the twenty patients were able to produce EMG increases sufficient to precipitate strong controlled muscle activity. The other three patients achieved similar success, but took a little longer. Although no follow-up data were provided and the report is sadly lacking in detail, improvement of this order in otherwise unresponsive patients has to be considered encouraging.

Impressive results, at least for some patients, were also reported by Johnson and Garton (1973). Ten hemiplegics with stable paralysis of the tibialis (lower leg) muscle were provided with EMG biofeedback from appropriately sited needle electrodes while they attempted ankle flexion. Three laboratory training sessions were provided, supplemented with home practice twice daily for between two and sixteen weeks. Four of the patients made remarkable recoveries, improving their ankle flexion and gait sufficiently to walk without a leg brace. Three of the remainder showed fair improvement in muscle functioning, while the others gained minimal or no benefit.

Brudny et al. (1976) employed EMG biofeedback from surface electrodes with 114 patients who exhibited a variety of neuromuscular disorders. Included in the total were forty-five patients diagnosed as suffering from hemiparesis. Whereas the term hemiplegia in usually reserved for instances of unambiguous paralysis, hemiparesis denotes weakness and a relative difficulty in moving a particular muscle or limb. It signifies slightly less severe impairment. However, the source remains the same; stroke is again the most common cause. As in previous studies, the conditions of Brudny et al.'s patients had proved resistant to conventional therapy. EMG biofeedback was provided during the attempted contraction and relaxation of affected musculature. In some cases, biofeedback was given simultaneously from two opposing muscle sites, in order to encourage coordinated movements. Sessions were three to five times weekly for a period of eight to twelve weeks. Clinical assessment revealed substantial improvement in twenty-seven out of the thirty-nine patients suffering from upper extremity dysfunction. Twenty of these still showed improvement at follow-up examinations conducted anywhere between three months and three years after treatment. Of the six remaining patients who required lower extremity treatment, three demonstrated substantial improvements in ambulation and gait.

Given such strong indications of efficacy, it is again unfortunate that so few controlled investigations have been conducted. To date, only three studies have included comparison groups or conditions of the sort necessary for proper evaluation.

Basmajian et al. (1975) allocated twenty hemiplegic patients to one of two groups. Ankle flexion was the target response and patients in one group received exercise and gait training. Patients in the other group were treated similarly during the first half of each 40-minute session; in the second half, however, EMG feedback from the tibialis muscle was provided during exercise attempts. In all, fifteen sessions of treatment were provided, spread over five weeks. Clinical examination indicated that both groups benefited in terms of strength and the range of movement possible. The biofeedback group, however, displayed average gains in these two indices that were approximately double those of the exercise group. There were substantial improvements in gait for some but not all patients, and three of the biofeedback patients were able to walk without a leg brace. At follow up, on average nine weeks after treatment, improvement was still evident. While this study is commendably sophisticated, a number of considerations weaken its status as a testament to the relative efficacy of biofeedback (Fish et al. 1976). First of all, statistical analysis reveals that, of the outcome measures, only strength reliably distinguishes the two groups. Second, the patients in the two groups differed with regard to the duration of their hemiplegia; patients in the exercise group averaged forty-five months since strokes, whereas those in the biofeedback group averaged only twenty-three months. Since it is generally acknowledged that the more chronic the condition, the poorer the prognosis, the biofeedback group might have been expected to improve more, regardless of treatment. Finally, the groups also differed with regard to the timing of follow-up; exercise group patients were assessed on average seven weeks after treatment, whereas the average lag for the biofeedback group was eleven weeks. However, this discrepancy was, if anything, likely to favour the exercise group.

Although these imbalances in group constitution and follow-up might be considered to cancel each other out, the results of statistical comparison leave nagging doubts; on only one of the two main outcome measures did biofeedback afford certain advantage. While this is far from failure, it is hardly sufficient to establish biofeedback's general effectiveness relative to more traditional treatment programmes.

Mroczek et al. (1978) also compared EMG biofeedback with a variety of physical therapies in the treatment of hemiplegic patients. In all, nine patients were studied; for seven of these the target response was contraction of the wrist extensor muscles, for one it was contraction of the biceps, and for the final patient, therapy aimed at inhibiting biceps activity. In the biofeedback condition, patients were instructed to use the EMG feedback display to contract and relax the affected muscles alternatively. The other condition consisted of muscle manipulation, exercise and relaxation. Following four sessions of baseline assessment, all nine patients received both treatments. However, treatment order was counterbalanced. Five of the patients received four weeks of EMG biofeedback, with three sessions per week, followed by four weeks of physical therapy, again three sessions weekly. For the remaining four patients, treatment order was reversed and physical therapy preceded biofeedback. While both treatments effected significant improvements in EMG activity in the target muscles and in the active range of movement, no reliable treatment differences emerged. However, the first treatment order, i.e. biofeedback followed by physical therapy, produced greater overall gains in EMG activity than the second treatment order. This was not so with regard to range of movement, where both orders yielded reliable and equivalent benefit. Overall, then, Mzoczek et al.'s data suggest that biofeedback is no more clinically effective than a less technologically-intensive alternative. However, it should be pointed out that their physical therapy involved decidely more patient-therapist contact. Given the pervasive influence of attention as a placebo, differences of this sort are likely to be of consequence.

Only one study so far has attempted placebo control. Lee et al. (1976) exposed eighteen hemiplegic patients on successive days to three treatment conditions: EMG biofeedback from the deficient deltoid muscle, false EMG feedback, and no feedback. The order of the condition was counterbalanced. Lee et al. observed no reliable differences between the conditions in terms of EMG activity; veridical EMG feedback was no more effective than false feedback in increasing EMG amplitude.

Further, older, less highly motivated patients improved more in terms of EMG activity than younger, more highly motivated patients, a result strikingly at odds with most clinical experience. While the use of false feedback in this context is to be lauded, this particular experiment suffers from a number of serious weaknesses. First no clinical outcome measures were reported. Second, only about five minutes of biofeedback treatment were provided; this is hardly sufficient to afford a proper test of efficacy. Third, the credibility of the false feedback provision was not assessed. Clearly, less flawed and more extensive study is required before the placebo issue can be resolved.

Peripheral nerve damage

In hemiplegia, we are dealing with muscle dysfunction arising from damage to the central nervous system. However, muscle paralysis and deficiencies can also result from damage to peripheral nerve fibres, either through accident or disease. Several researchers have now addressed the question of whether debilities derived from peripheral nerve impairment respond to treatment with EMG biofeedback.

In the earliest study of this sort, Marinacci and Horande (1960) treated seven patients suffering from a variety of neuromuscular problems. Needle electrodes were inserted in the affected musculature and auditory EMG biofeedback was provided along with instructions to increase the feedback signal. The extent of the treatment varied from patient to patient, but all were able to increase EMG activity in the deficient muscles. In addition, Marinacci and Horande reported either a complete return to normal functioning or a substantial improvement in functioning for all seven patients. More specific detail was given in individual cases. Consider the example of a young man suffering from Bell's palsy, a facial paralysis of unknown origin. The patient had suffered complete paralysis of the right side of the face for six years. Needle electrodes recorded some residual activity in the paralysed orbicularis oris muscle surrounding the mouth. Biofeedback was provided from this site and the patient encouraged to increase the feedback signal. Within a week of regular treatment, the patient regained approximately 20 per cent of the voluntary contraction of both the orbicularis oris and the right frontalis muscles. Improvement continued and by the end of six months' treatment the patient had achieved a 40 per cent return of function.

Booker et al. (1969) reported on a single case of peripheral nerve damage. Part of the left temporal bone had been fractured, severing the facial nerve. Surgery had achieved partial re-innervation of the facial muscles, but the patient was still unable to control voluntarily the facial muscle on the left side or blink his left eye. EMG biofeedback from the affected side was given initially to aid the patient in increasing and decreasing muscle movements. Once voluntary increases and decreases has been established, feedback from both sides of the face was provided and the patient attempted to match activity from the deficient side with that from the normal side. Four one-hour sessions were held weekly for three weeks, followed by home practice in front of a mirror and supplementary laboratory feedback sessions. With treatment, facial muscle strength increased as did facial coordination and symmetry, although some asymmetry persisted during facial expressions, such as smiling, and during speech. Partial loss of these therapeutic gains was evident at four months follow-up. However, three days of further biofeedback training were sufficient to re-establish control.

Kukulka et al. (1975) treated three patients who had suffered damage to various hand tendons and had just undergone surgery to repair the damaged tendons. Treatment was three times weekly for three weeks and each session conisted of a whirlpool bath, physiotherapy and finally twenty minutes of flexor muscle EMG biofeedback as various hand and finger exercises were attempted.

The aim of treatment was to re-establish the mobility of the finger joints. Kukulka et al. reported that all three patients achieved marked improvement in the active range of their finger movements, and in some instances finger mobility returned to normal levels.

Finally, Jankel (1978) presented the case of a woman with Bell's palsy. The patient had suffered this condition for fifteen years; right-sided smiling was impaired, the right eyelid was closed and the eye rotated upward and laterally, and the jaw was displaced. Treatment consisted of surface EMG biofeedback from the paralysed side of the face. The patient was required to match this feedback to signals derived from the normal side of the face. Daily sessions were conducted for a total of three weeks. Both EMG levels and facial movements substantially improved with treatment. Jaw position was more normal, the eye was no longer abnormally rotated, and facial expressions, such as smiling, were symmetrical.

Given these interesting and provocative case reports, it is unfortunate that controlled studies have not as yet been conducted in this area. They could well establish EMG boifeedback as a valuable innovation in the treatment of muscular disorders arising from peripheral nerve damage.

Spasmodic torticollis

The major symptom of spasmodic torticollis comprises an extreme rotation of the head to one side, giving the impression of someone continuously looking over their shoulder. Also known as wryneck, the aberrant posture is generally fairly sustained, although spasms and jerks may be superimposed. Clearly the condition reflects abnormal activity in the neck muscles, but the exact neural mechanisms remain a mystery. Certainly, the head rotation is usually resistant to attempts at manual correction, but, strangely, the symptoms disappear during sleep, only to return on waking. The untreated prognosis is almost invariably poor; there is little spontaneous remission and the condition usually becomes a permanent disability. Neurosurgical treatment has been tried but the success rate is low.

EMG biofeedback has now been applied with several patients and, given the untreated prognosis, the results are reasonably encouraging. Cleeland (1973) treated ten torticollis patients. Auditory EMG biofeedback was provided while they attempted to relax the affected neck muscles and normalize head posture. In addition, mild electric shocks were delivered to the finger when muscle spasms occurred. The number of treatment sessions ranged from 6–23, with an average of 11. Follow-up assessment was performed between one and forty months after treatment; the average length of follow-up was eighteen months. Outcome was evaluated in terms of spasm frequency and a three-point rating scale of improvement. Spasm frequency dropped on average from a pretreatment level of 54 per five minutes to 24 per five minutes after treatment. The gains seemed to be reasonably long-lasting. At follow-up, three of the patients were rated as markedly improved and three as moderately so. While Cleeland's results are impressive, it is unfortunate that the independent contributions of EMG biofeedback and shock delivery cannot be determined. As such, it must remain a possibility that the shock component of the treatment package, and not biofeedback, constituted the effective element.

Brudny et al.'s (1976) study included forty-eight spasmodic torticollis patients. Surface EMG biofeedback was provided from the affected neck muscles and patients attended sessions three to five times weekly for between eight to ten weeks. Follow-up conducted between three months and three years after treatment indicated sustained improvement in nineteen out of the forty-eight. Improvement included large reductions in EMG activity in the affected muscles, the head posture returning to normal, or the patient becoming able to control occasional torticollis episodes.

Although both these studies strongly suggest that EMG biofeedback can indeed bring benefit to patients suffering from spasmodic torticollis, science, as always, requires that final judgement be waived until properly controlled studies have been conducted.

Cerebral palsy

Yet another area of application in this context is cerebral palsy. Cerebral palsy denotes a range of sensory-motor disturbances caused by non-progressive brain-damage sustained usually prenatally or at birth. Common are disorders of posture and gait, as well as bizarre and stereotyped patterns of movement. The particular symptoms depend on the location and extent of the brain damage. Biofeedback has been applied in an attempt to improve posture and gait, and to eliminate abnormal movement patterns.

Harris et al. (1974) used movement-sensitive transducers to supply feedback of aberrant posture and movement. Two devices were used. On one, the sensors were mounted on a helmet and feedback provided as a series of clicks which increased as the patient's head deviated from normal posture. On the second, the sensors relayed information on wrist and elbow rotation; feedback, in this case, took the form of an unpleasant noise whenever arm movements exceeded normal limits. The patients were eighteen cerebral palsied school children who were treated three to seven times weekly for between two and twelve months. All children with the head control device improved head stability: before training a normal head position could be maintained for only a few seconds, whereas after treatment this increased to more than five minutes. Similarly, all those children treated with the arm position monitor increased the smoothness, accuracy and range of their arm movements.

Wooldridge and Russell (1976) also used movement sensitive headgear to provide audiovisual feedback of head position to twelve cerebral palsied children. Feedback was provided when the head moved out of the upright. For some children supplementary feedback facilities were employed; these included clocks, cable cars, race tracks, television sets, and radios which would switch off when abnormal head positions were assumed. The frequency and duration of the training differed from child to child; the location of the training was also varied in order to optimize generalization. Outcome was evaluated by clinical examination. Three of the patients showed no noteworthy functional improvement, six demonstrated consistent improvement in the presence of feedback but little when feedback was removed, and three showed improvement that was maintained in the absence of feedback. Much the same picture emerged at follow-up observation, up to three months after treatment.

Finley et al. (1976) treated six cerebral palsied patients with frontalis EMG biofeedback in an attempt to improve speech and motor control. Following baseline assessment, twelve weeks of training were given over a period of six weeks. All six patients managed some reduction in EMG activity; for five of the six the reductions were statistically reliable. On average, frontalis EMG decreased from 29 microvolts initially to 13 microvolts by the end of training. In addition, all six patients improved in terms of movement control. Improvement rates ranged from 71–92 per cent; the average was 82 per cent. Four of the six also performed substantially better on a speech test following treatment; the average increase for these four was 74 per cent.

In a subsequent study of four cerebral palsied children, Finley et al. (1977) again used auditory and visual feedback of frontalis EMG activity. Following a clinical evaluation of speech and fine motor control, the children received biofeedback training for six weeks, with two sessions per week. Their speech and motor abilities were subsequently re-evaluated. There were then six weeks of no treatment, followed once more by a clinical examination. Finally, the children received another eight biweekly sessions of biofeedback training, at the end of which their speech and movement control were again evaluated. Frontalis EMG levels decreased across the twelve initial sessions of feedback, but rose during the no-treatment phase. However, with the second session of feedback, EMG levels once again decreased. By the end of training, levels had fallen to 14 microvolts on average from an initial average of 22 microvolts. Improvements in speech and movement control followed a similar course; after the no-treatment phase there was some loss of the gains apparent following the initial bout of biofeedback. Again, however, substantial clinical improvements were evident with the second period of feedback. Overall, a combined index of speech and movement control, based on four-point ratings during a variety of tasks (where 1 = best performance, 4 = poorest performance) decreased from 191 units initially to 92 by the end of treatment.

Once again, the results of these studies are encouraging. Sufficient clinical gains have been demonstrated to commend more controlled and hence more definitive study.

Conclusions

Given the character of the clinical conditions considered in this chapter, biofeedback emerges as a promising addition or even alternative to more conventional therapies. A substantial number of severely disabled patients have shown impressive improvement following treatment. Unfortunately, nearly all of the studies reviewed lack the control conditions necessary for unqualified pronouncements of efficacy. Nevertheless, since many of the reports concern patients whose disabilities had proved resistant to previous therapeutic intervention, interpretations of positive results with biofeedback in terms of simple improvement with time would seem unlikely, as would suggestions that biofeedback may be no more effective than already existing, simpler alternatives. However, some qualifications are in order. While the results of the two studies which compared EMG biofeedback directly with conventional physical therapy might be considered favourable to feedback, in one of them biofeedback actually effected no greater improvement, although it admittedly demanded less therapist-patient contact (Mroczek et al. 1978). In the other study the advantage of feedback was restricted to only one outcome measure (Basmajian et al. 1975). Clearly, further studies of this sort are necessary in order to establish properly the relative merits of biofeedback in this context. In addition, the placebo issue still has to be confronted: the one study that did so directly by deploying false feedback (Lee et al. 1976) contained too many weaknesses to provide a satisfactory answer.

Chapter 7

Epilepsy

EEG activity

For over fifty years it has been known that when recording electrodes are placed on the human scalp, they register a fluctuating pattern of electrical activity. However, while it is reasonable to presume that this brain wave, or electroencephalograph (EEG) activity, reflects the workings of the brain, the precise nature of its relationship to brain functioning remains unclear. Nevertheless, a number of distinct wave-forms or rhythms have now been isolated from the general electrical mosaic. The most common rhythms observed in waking adults are alpha and beta waves. Alpha waves, ranging in frequency from 8–13 cycles per second (Hz), are observed most commonly in relaxed individuals at rest with their eyes closed. Beta waves are faster than alpha waves at 14–30 Hz. They appear to accompany states of relative alertness; for example, when a relaxed individual is suddenly stimulated the prevailing alpha rhythm is normally replaced by beta activity. The slowest waves are delta waves; this classification is reserved for waves of less than 4 Hz. Delta waves are a salient feature of the EEG when an adult is asleep, but they are rare after waking up. Finally, the term theta is applied to waves in the 4–7 Hz frequency band. A normal component in the EEG of children, theta waves become rarer with emerging adulthood, although they often accompany episodes of emotional distress in adults. While these are the major traditional categories of brain-wave frequencies, further delineation within these broad bands is often undertaken. In addition, it should be emphasized that at any given moment the adult EEG is unlikely to comprise waves of only one sort. Rather, it is the case that one wave-form will be more predominant than the others. Finally, wave-form is also to some extent a function of the electrodes' recording site as well as the patient's psychological state. For example, alpha waves, are observed best over the posterior, occipital regions of the scalp.

Epilepsy

In a number of neurological conditions, the EEG displays unusual or abnormal features. Undoubtedly the most dramatic departures from the normal occur with epilepsy. In epilepsy, a group of nerve cells in the brain suddenly discharge abnormally. These discharges are readily registered on an EEG trace, although their precise form and extent can vary enormously; EEG recording thus provides an invaluable diagnostic service.

Just as the electrical manifestations of epilepsy vary, so too do the behavioural symptoms: from the complete loss of consciousness and dramatic muscular spasms and contortions that often epitomize grand mal epileptic fits at one end of the spectrum, to the transient and minimal muscle twitches that characterize some petit mal attacks. Observable changes vary not only in terms of severity, but also in terms of specificity. While epilepsy frequently involves widespread behavioural disruption, occasionally the effects are fairly circumscribed, with only focal areas of sensation or movement being disturbed. Finally, the environmental antecedents of epileptic attacks are equally various; the most commonly cited are emotional stress, lack of sleep, overexertion and alcohol abuse. In some cases fairly specific stimuli seem to act as triggers; flickering lights, television and music have all been indicated.

Epilepsy is usually treated by means of anticonvulsive drugs. However, they often prove less than adequate. Like most drugs they are not without side effects and it is estimated that some 25 per cent of epileptic patients respond poorly to even very large doses of anticonvulsant medication (Kuhlman and Kaplan 1979). Brain surgery has occasionally been undertaken as a last resort. Neural connections, such as the corpus callosum which links the two hemispheres of the brain, have been severed to prevent the spread of crippling epileptic discharges, or the area around the suspected focus of the discharge has been surgically destroyed, as in some cases of temporal lobe epilepsy. However, radical brain surgery is hardly an ideal solution. While seizures are at least usually curtailed, if not totally eliminated, improvement is often bought at the expense of deficits in general functioning. Undoubtedly, some less risky alternative to drastic surgery is required for those patients who fail to benefit from anticonvulsant medication.

EEG biofeedback

One of biofeedback's earliest boasts was that it enabled people to control EEG activity voluntarily. In fact, it could be argued that much of the subsequent enthusiasm for biofeedback stemmed from this seemingly miraculous discovery (see Kamiya 1968). In addition, since epilepsy is characterized by abnormal problems of EEG activity, the application of biofeedback seemed the logical step. Several studies have now examined the efficacy of biofeedback in this context. Researchers have generally opted for one of three EEG rhythms: sensorimotor rhythm, alpha or mu.

Sensorimotor feedback

The majority of epilepsy research has deployed feedback

of what was regarded as the human analogue of animal sensorimotor rhythm (SMR); the elected frequency range is usually either 12–14 Hz or 12–16 Hz. The rationale for this choice of rhythms was provided by the research of Sterman and his associates with cats (see Sterman 1973). The main findings can be briefly summarized as follows: 12–16 Hz rhythm can be recorded from above the sensorimotor areas of cats' brains; its appearance is associated with the absence of movement and it is interrupted by movement; it can be enhanced by training and such training seems to increase the animals' resistance to seizures. These last two results probably warrant elaboration. When cats are deprived of food and then offered milk on the appearance of SMR, they show substantial increases in SMR incidence. In addition, cats so trained to enhance SMR display a higher seizure threshold to the convulsant drug, monomethylhydrazine, than untrained cats.

These data were considered sufficiently compelling for Sterman and Friar (1972) to deploy SMR biofeedback with an epileptic patient; the outcome of this enterprise together with the data from three subsequent patients were reported by Sterman et al. (1974). All four patients had long histories of epilepsy. In spite of anticonvulsant medication, seizure rates before biofeedback training ranged from two per month to eight per day. Feedback was geared to enhance SMR (12–14 Hz) activity, and patients received at least three training sessions per week for between six and eighteen months. For three of the patients biofeedback training was interrupted part way for a period of nine weeks. With training, patients showed some increase in SMR, plus quite a marked decrease in abnormal slow wave activity, although the effects disappeared with the interruption of feedback training. Seizure activity decreased substantially from the pretraining range to 0.05 per month to three per day. Overall, this represented a 66 per cent improvement in seizure incidence. With training interrupted, however, seizure rates more or less reverted to pretraining levels. Given the extent of the improvement with biofeedback, it is unfortunate that no systematic follow-up data are available. Nevertheless, the overall outcome was encouraging; SMR biofeedback clearly merited further study.

Finley (1974, 1976, 1977) has reported on a single epileptic boy subjected to much the same treatment regime. The boy had a history of frequent and severe seizures, averaging between 80–100 seizures per day. Biofeedback was given to facilitate SMR and to inhibit 4–7 Hz slow wave activity. In all, more than 180 sessions of training were undertaken over a period of approximately one year. When the patient was well into training, Finley introduced a period of non-contingent, i.e. false, feedback. With biofeedback, the patient managed to enhance SMR activity and reduce the incidence of slow waves. With the introduction of false feedback there was something of a return to the pretraining EEG pattern. Substantial clinical effects were also evident. Seizure rate dropped from a pretraining average level of eight per hour to less than one per hour by the end of training. Interestingly, this improvement in seizure rate was still apparent during the false feedback phase, although there is evidence to suggest that the severity of seizures increased with the introduction of non-contingent feedback. At follow-up, five months after treatment, the improvements in seizure rate were largely maintained. However, some increase in the severity of the attack was again noted. Clearly, the false feedback condition employed by Finley offers better control for non-specific or placebo effects than Sterman et al.'s device of simply interrupting treatment. Consequently, it is worth noting that while some relapse was observed with the interruption of training, false feedback had much less of an impact.

Lubar and his associates (Lubar 1977; Lubar and Bahler 1976; Seifert and Lubar 1975) also reported positive results for patients trained simultaneously to enhance SMR and reduce slow wave activity. In all, twelve patients were exposed to this style of biofeedback treatment. Patients attended for three sessions per week, and training was continued for up to thirty months. Physiological data are available only for eight patients; with training six of them managed some enhancement of SMR activity. However, all bar one of the full complement of patients registered improvements in seizure activity and/or severity. While no systematic follow-up was conducted, Lubar temporarily interrupted the training of three patients; seizure activity increased as a consequence.

Kaplan's (1975) results contrast markedly with those considered up to now. Two patients with long histories of epilepsy were provided with biofeedback to enhance SMR activity. Training was conducted three times weekly for a period of between three and four months. Not only were no EEG changes observed, but patients derived little or no clinical benefit; seizure rates remained at pretraining levels. However, there are notable differences between Kaplan's study and those reviewed previously. First of all, Kaplan's patients received less training than patients in the other studies. Second, whereas Finley and Lubar offered feedback for slow wave activity suppression in addition to the usual SMR provision, Kaplan relied solely on SMR feedback. Finally, and most important, all three previously cited studies used an inhibit circuit to prevent the delivery of feedback of SMR activity when it occurred in the presence of abnormal EEG activity characteristic of epilepsy. As Kuhlman and Kaplan (1979) argued, this facility probably affords specific feedback for the suppression of such abnormal activity. Clinical improvement, they claimed, might have had more to do with this agency, than with the provision of SMR biofeedback *per se*.

Kuhlman and Allison (1977) did not use an inhibit circuit when exploring the efficacy of biofeedback of a somewhat broader EEG frequency band (9–14 Hz). This band obviously encompasses the 12–14 Hz SMR range. Five patients whose seizures were poorly controlled by anticonvulsive drugs were exposed to both contingent and non-contingent feedback. Contingent feedback was introduced following an initial phase of non-contingent feedback; false feedback was subsequently reinstated before a final training phase with veridical biofeedback. Patients attended approximately three sessions per week for a period of around six months. Although biofeedback failed either to enhance activity in either the 9–14 Hz band or the more circumscribed SMR range, or to suppress abnormal low-frequency (3–6 Hz) activity, three of the five patients improved noticeably in terms of seizure activity. In fact, for two of these three, seizure activity decreased by some 60 per cent from pretraining levels. Kulhman and Allisons' (1977) results clearly indicate that clinical gains can be achieved without an inhibit circuit. However, at the same time, their data raise questions about the source of these gains, since they occurred in the absence of observed changes in EEG. While an explanation in terms of placebo immediately springs to mind, Kuhlman and Allisons' finding, that the three patients who eventually improved derived little benefit from the initial false feedback, argues against it.

In a recent study, Sterman and Macdonald (1978) also observed substantial clinical gains in the absence of changes in SMR activity. Four epileptic patients received biofeedback training simultaneously to enhance 12–15 Hz SMR activity and suppress frequencies in the 6–9 Hz range. Periods of laboratory training were interspersed with home practice. The study comprised three phases. In phase 1. biofeedback training was as described above; in phase 2, the aims were reversed and patients attempted to suppress SMR and enhance the slower wave activity; in phase 3, the initial contingencies were reinstated and patients once again tried to enhance SMR and suppress activity in the 6–9 Hz frequency range. Each phase of training, including the home practice component, lasted approximately three months. An inhibit circuit was used throughout to prevent the delivery of feedback during abnormal EEG activity. Seizure activity was decreased markedly during phase 3; an average decrease of some 74 per cent was observed. However, there was no evidence of voluntary SMR control. Nevertheless, Sterman and Macdonald did note decreases in the amount of abnormal activity present in the EEG profiles.

The results of these last two studies seriously question the existence of a link between epilepsy and EEG activity in the 12–14 Hz range. Data subsequently provided by Kuhlman (see Kuhlman 1978) cast even further doubt. Making use of the criteria that identity feline SMR (i.e. its rhythmic quality, its localization in the sensorimotor areas, its association with the absence of movement) Kuhlman scanned the human EEG spectrum for activity with equivalent characteristics. The activity which best conformed to these criteria lay not in the 12–14 Hz frequency range, but in the alpha 8–13 Hz band. In fact, it corresponded in profile to the mu rhythm described originally by Gastaut (1952). Given that the guiding objective of biofeedback training has been to modify the human analogue of feline SMR, it would seem that researchers have been consistently focusing on the wrong rhythm.

Clearly, a number of epileptics have improved markedly with SMR feedback. Others, however, have gained little benefit. Further, there would appear to be no orderly relationship between changes in SMR and improvements in clinical condition. Some of those experiencing a reduction in seizure rate have failed to control SMR, while for others SMR control was without clinical consequence. Finally, Kuhlman's (1978) results seriously undermine the whole rationale for SMR biofeedback.

Alpha feedback

Some researchers have opted for alpha rather than sensorimotor feedback. While no specific rationale for alpha feedback in the treatment of epilepsy has been formulated, the choice is not wholly haphazard, as the earliest successes in voluntary EEG control involved alpha activity. Three studies offer indications of the efficacy of alpha feedback in this context.

Johnson and Meyer (1974) provided data from a single case study. The patient had a long history of epilepsy and displayed a pretraining seizure rate of three per month. Training comprised three parts: in part 1, the patient received relaxation training for two weeks; in part 2, EMG biofeedback was provided for seven sessions; in part 3, the patients received alpha feedback, a combination of alpha-theta feedback, and theta feedback in a phased sequence for thirty-six sessions. In all, treatment lasted about twelve months. Over the treatment period, seizure rate dropped from the pretraining level to around 1.5 per month. This gain was maintained at three-month follow-up; the patient reported experiencing no more than one seizure per month in the three months following treatment. Although these data look promising, it is difficult to determine the active element in this rather complex treatment package. There is certainly no justification for presuming that alpha biofeedback was the sole or even main effective component.

A similar difficulty surrounds the single case study reported by Rouse et al. (1975). Before biofeedback training, the patient experienced seizures approximately once per week. Training consisted of one week of feedback of 8–13 Hz activity, followed by four months of 9–11 Hz feedback. Thus training was geared initially to enhance alpha activity and then subsequently switched to focus that activity around the 10 Hz frequency mark. In addition, the patient was encouraged to practise meditation at home, both during biofeedback training and after the completion of training. Biofeedback evidently effected the desired change in EEG. Further, the patient reported a complete absence of seizures during the last one-and-a-half months of training, and remained seizure-free during the eighteen months of follow-up. While these results are again encouraging, it is difficult to attribute relief to the alpha feedback facility with any measure of confidence. Among other things it remains possible that clinical improvement owed more to repeated meditation than to biofeedback.

Cabral and Scott (1976) treated three patients whose seizures were precipitated by specific anxiety-provoking stimuli. For two of the patients, treatment consisted of three months of alpha biofeedback followed by three months of relaxation training. For the remaining patient, treatment order was reversed: alpha feedback followed the relaxation training. Throughout, treatment was administered in the presence of the sorts of stimuli which were associated with epileptic attacks. Both treatments resulted in improvements in abnormal EEG activity. In addition, although all three patients reported reductions in seizures activity, no reliable differences in treatment effectiveness were found. Finally, follow-up evaluation at fifteen months revealed that the improvements were largely maintained.

In conclusion, alpha biofeedback as a treatment for epilepsy can muster only the most marginal support. Very few patients have been studied and improvements in seizure activity can, without exception, be attributed to factors other than the provision of alpha feedback. Only one study has compared alpha biofeedback directly with another mode of treatment. While the study is somewhat modest in scope, biofeedback was observed to be no more effective than standard training in relaxation.

Mu feedback

As indicated previously, Kuhlman's (1978) investigations implicate mu rather than 12–16 Hz activity as the human equivalent of feline SMR. The mu rhythm, which is generally considered to be within a 9–11 Hz frequency band, has a characteristic 'comb' appearance and tends to appear on the EEG record in bursts. It is apparently more frequent in the EEG of younger subjects. Unfortunately, to date, only two studies have deployed mu biofeedback in the treatment of epilepsy.

Kaplan (1975) presented three epileptic patients with biofeedback for increases in 6–12 Hz activity, a range which encompasses the mu rhythm. Sessions were three times weekly and training was continued for between five and six months. Two of the three patients demonstrated significant reductions in seizure frequency with training. However, the source of these clinical gains remains unclear, since none of the patients managed to enhance mu activity.

More recently, Quy et al. (1979) compared the efficacy of feedback to enhance 8–10 Hz mu activity and feedback to increase 12–16 Hz SMR activity. Two other comparison conditions were included: feedback to suppress abnormal high voltage EEG activity, and random, non-contingent feedback. Three chronic epileptic patients were exposed to the following four training conditions in turn. In condition 1 feedback was given to enhance SMR. Training was continued for twenty-four weeks, with approximately two sessions per week. Condition 2 lasted fourteen weeks with feedback geared to enhance activity in the mu range. The feedback facility used in conditions 1 and 2 included an inhibit circuit designed to suppress abnormal high voltage activity. In condition 3, the independent contribution of this inhibit circuit was evaluated. In effect, patients received ten weeks of feedback geared solely to suppress abnormal EEG activity. Finally, in condition 4, patients received ten weeks of false feedback. None of the patients were informed that feedback in this instance was false and none guessed the deception. The data indicated that while all three patients experienced a significant reduction in seizure rate by the end of the study, improvement was not associated with any particular training condition. For example, only one of the patients displayed a significant decrease in seizure rate in condition 1. In addition, this improvement was not associated with any change in SMR;

it was the remaining two patients who demonstrated SMR enhancement. A second patient improved most during condition 2, and the third patient benefited most during condition 3. Finally, the introduction of false feedback did not result in any loss of improvement.

Taken together, these two studies indicate that changes in mu (or for that matter SMR) are not critical for seizure reduction. Both studies strongly imply that clinical benefit arises from non-specific factors in the therapeutic milieu.

Feedback of other EEG frequencies

Feedback of frequencies both above and below the usual ranges selected for attention has now received preliminary study. Wyler et al. (1976) trained four epileptic patients to enhance EEG frequencies above 14 Hz. Three to five sessions of biofeedback training were provided weekly for between eight to sixteen weeks. With training, all four patients managed to increase the amount of high frequency activity in the EEG and two of the four displayed a decrease in seizure rate. The remaining two experienced a reduction in seizure severity, but an increase in the frequency of the less severe seizures. These improvements were evident only on the days of feedback training; on days with no training, seizure activity more or less reverted to pretraining levels.

More recently, Cott et al. (1979) provided seven epileptics with biofeedback for suppression of the 4–7 Hz frequency band. In addition, four of the patients simultaneously received feedback for increases in the 12–14 Hz range. Sessions were twice weekly for six weeks. Three of the patients managed to enhance 12–14 Hz activity and five achieved reductions in 4–7 Hz activity. Further, five of the seven patients recorded decreases in seizure frequency. However, clinical gains were not linked in any simple manner to EEG control. For example, the two patients who experienced no improvement in seizure rate, successfully curtailed 4–7 Hz frequencies. In contrast, another patient derived substantial clinical benefit but showed no reduction in 4–7 Hz activity.

While these two studies are interesting in that they appear to demonstrate therapeutic gains with fairly modest amounts of biofeedback training, they are unable to link these gains to changes in a particular EEG frequency band. Further, in the absence of follow-up, the durability of the clinical effects remains open to doubt. Wyler et al's observation, that seizure activity returned to pretraining levels on days without biofeedback, inevitably fuels that suspicion that the benefit may have been short-lived.

Conclusions

Clearly a number of epileptic patients have now gained some measure of relief from EEG biofeedback. However, the precise source of the clinical effects remains something of a mystery. There is certainly little to suggest that improvement arises from the control of any particular EEG frequency range. Reductions in seizure activity have been observed with a variety of biofeedback provisions: SMR, mu, alpha, and slow wave biofeedback. In fact, no specific feedback facility would seem to be any more effective than any other. In addition, therapeutic benefit and success at EEG control, whatever the target frequency, correlate very imperfectly. Clinical effects have been observed in the absence of voluntary EEG control, and, conversely, EEG changes have been achieved without improvements in seizure activity. Further, the theoretical bases for the various biofeedback arrangements applied to epilepsy are either poorly developed or at odds with subsequent empirical evidence. While SMR biofeedback embarked from a reasonably well-elaborated theoretical rationale, Kuhlman's (1978) data cast serious doubts on the central presumption that human 12–16 Hz EEG activity is analogous to feline SMR; if anything, it would now seem that the human equivalent is the mu rhythm.

In the end, what remains is the suspicion that EEG biofeedback exerts a fairly non-specific influence and that many of the clinical effects are best attributed to expectancy of relief and the placebo of a superficially impressive and technically-sophisticated therapy. Even here, though, there are counter-indications. While the introduction of false feedback in a number of studies has failed to compromise gains already made (as in Quy et al. 1979), Kuhlman and Allisons' failure to find clinical improvement in the initial false feedback phase of their study argues against explanations in terms of placebo effects. However, it is worth pointing out that epileptic patients generally require fairly extended exposure to biofeedback before they derive much benefit. It is possible that Kuhlman and Allisons' false feedback phase was too short, and that improvements would have appeared with longer exposure to false feedback. Hopefully, future research will address this and the many other questions posed by EEG biofeedback. Certainly, enough severely epileptic patients have already been helped to suggest that something efficacious is at work and that the active therapeutic element is worth isolating.

Chapter 8

Fear and anxiety

Introduction

Biofeedback has been advertised frequently as a remedy for severe anxiety and debilitating fears or phobias. Since both specific phobias and more diffuse, general anxiety states are usually characterized by symptoms of marked physiological upheaval (elevated HR, increased muscle tension, etc.), a treatment which aspires to provide physiological self-control would seem at first glance to be a good bet. In fact, many of the conventional therapeutic approaches to fear and anxiety (progressive relaxation, systematic desensitization, etc.) presume to effect changes in biological reaction or disposition. In addition, many of the psychological theories of emotion (see Mandler 1975; Schachter 1966, 1971) accord a central role to physiological disturbance. Changes in biological functioning are regarded by many psychologists not merely as expressions of emotional states, but as crucial determinants of subjective feeling; stated simply, they consider that it is the awareness of interal physiological upheaval in a particular circumstance that sustains the feelings of fear and anxiety. If such theories are correct, biofeedback, by affording physiological self-regulation, should effect a change in subjective state.

A number of different biofeedback facilities have now been applied to anxiety sufferers. The most popular have been EMG and HR biofeedback. The patients selected for treatment have also varied, ranging from those with specific phobias to those exhibiting much more pervasive anxiety reactions.

EMG biofeedback

Wickramasekera (1972b) was the first to apply EMG biofeedback in this context. Frontalis EMG feedback was employed as a supplement to systematic desensitization with a woman who displayed a phobia of examinations. Two initial sessions of biofeedback were provided to facilitate relaxation. Systematic desensitization was then undertaken, during which she viewed video-recorded, examination-related scenes arranged as an increasingly anxiety-provoking series. The patient was required to terminate a scene whenever frontalis muscle tension, as signalled by biofeedback, rose to a specified high level. Basic experience with systematic desensitization techniques indicates that, over repeated sessions, increasingly threatening stimuli come to be tolerated. In Wickramasekera's study, EMG levels decreased over the training sessions and, by the end of treatment, the patient was able to complete the previously distressing examination successfully. The patient reported further examination achievement at short-term follow-up.

Budzynski and Stoyva (1973) also provided anecdotal evidence of success in treating anxiety with this marriage of frontalis EMG biofeedback and systematic desensitization. Reeves and Mealiea (1975) applied the same sort of treatment package to three patients with phobias about flying. In the initial phases of the study, EMG biofeedback was provided to promote relaxation. In the trial phase, the patients received systematic desensitization aided by the relaxation facility. All three managed to decrease EMG levels: from a range of 7–8 mV before treatment to 2–3 mV after treatment. In addition, following treatment they all managed to fly commercially on several occasions, experiencing only the most minimal anxiety.

Although these reports look promising, they are hardly sufficient to establish the efficacy of EMG biofeedback. After all, numerous studies attest to the effectiveness of systematic desensitization *per se*. While Budzynski and Stoyva claimed that EMG biofeedback added to the effectiveness of systematic desensitization, not nearly enough detail is presented to evaluate this claim.

Raskin et al. (1973) examined the effectiveness of EMG biofeedback *per se* in reducing anxiety. Ten patients were provided with frontalis EMG biofeedback to facilitate relaxation. Once they had achieved sustained decreases in forehead muscle tension, laboratory sessions without biofeedback were interspersed among those with feedback to promote generalization. In addition, patients were encouraged to practise their relaxation skills at home. The training period lasted six weeks on average. All patients managed substantial reductions in frontalis EMG activity; with training, EMG eventually dropped to between one-half and one-eighth of pretraining levels. However, subjective ratings of mood revealed that only four of the ten patients experienced any relief from anxiety. In addition, although these four could now manage, when alone, to reduce their levels of anxiety, they were at a loss to prevent the onset of anxiety attacks. Further, only three of the four indicated any success in dealing with anxiety in everyday social situations. While these results are not particularly encouraging, it should be emphasized that Raskin et al.'s patients suffered from particularly severe anxiety that had failed to respond adequately to other sorts of therapy.

As indicated previously, data from uncontrolled studies are insufficient to establish therapeutic efficacy fully. Controlled experiments, in which the particular procedure of interest is compared with no treatment or with alternative treatments or, optimally, with a suitably contrived placebo condition, are essential. A number of researchers have now attempted controlled investigations of EMG biofeedback for anxiety problems.

Canter et al. (1975) allocated twenty-eight anxiety

patients to one of two treatment groups. The fourteen patients in group 1 received between ten and twenty-five sessions of frontalis EMG biofeedback; group 2 patients spent similar amounts of time practising a modified version of progressive relaxation. Both groups displayed significant decreases in forehead muscle tension. For group 1, tension, on average, dropped from an initial baseline level of 29.0 mV to 12.8 during the final sessions, while for group 2, tension dropped from 32.7 mV to 24.4 mV. Anxiety levels, assessed by both patient and therapist, showed improvements in twelve of the fourteen patients treated with biofeedback, and in seven of the fourteen who practised relaxation. Although no statistical analyses are reported on these clinical data, they would nonetheless seem to indicate that biofeedback is of more value than some relaxation procedures in countering anxiety.

Townsend et al. (1975) also reported positive evidence for EMG biofeedback, this time relative to group psychotherapy. Thirty patients suffering from chronic anxiety were assigned either to frontalis EMG biofeedback or to group psychotherapy. A total of nine feedback sessions were provided spread over three weeks. Those allocated to group psychotherapy attended for sixteen relatively lengthy sessions, during which they took part in discussions of anxiety-provoking events. Scores on a standard anxiety questionnaire indicated marked improvements for the patients given biofeedback. The average anxiety score for the biofeedback group decreased to 43.8 from an initial value of 51.3. The patients exposed to group psychotherapy showed no such change; their initial and final average values were 40.9 and 41.8 respectively. While these data are indeed encouraging, it should be pointed out that the biofeedback patients would seem to have had higher initial anxiety levels, and consequently greater scope for improvement.

In contrast to the last two studies, the data provided by Jessup and Neufeld (1977) do little to commend biofeedback in this context. Twenty patients suffering from anxiety and depression were assigned to one of four groups. Group 1 received biofeedback training to reduce frontalis EMG levels, and group 2 were given autogenic training (see chapter four for a description). Patients in group 3 were told simply to relax, but given no formal relaxation training. Finally, group 4 patients received non-contingent, i.e. false, EMG feedback; they were informed that the biofeedback signal was designed as an aid to relaxation. Patients received four sessions of their designated treatment. Self-ratings of mood revealed improvements in anxiety only for groups 2 and 4. Patients in the EMG biofeedback group registered no such benefit. While biofeedback was particularly ineffective in this study, Jessup and Neufeld provided relatively few treatment sessions, and no reductions in forehead tension were, in fact, achieved. Biofeedback might have proved effective given more protracted training. At the same time, however, four treatment sessions were sufficient for both autogenic training and non-contingent feedback to effect clinical changes.

Beiman et al. (1978) compared EMG biofeedback with three different relaxation procedures: progressive relaxation, presented in person by a therapist, progressive relaxation, presented by tape, and a self-relaxation procedure based on transcendental meditation (see Benson 1975). Forty anxiety patients were divided among these four training conditions and subject to five sessions of their particular treatment. Both the clinical and physiological data indicated no advantage for EMG biofeedback over the other treatments. Rather progressive relaxation, with the live therapist, effected the most pronounced changes in physiology (HR as well as EMG) and the greatest improvement in anxiety. While biofeedback is again poorly supported, this study is also open to the criticism that training was too limited.

Clearly, the application of frontalis EMG biofeedback in the treatment of anxiety cannot attract unqualified pronouncements of efficacy. Although the results of earlier uncontrolled studies are almost uniformly encouraging, subsequent controlled experiments paint a decidedly less consistent picture. Whereas Canter et al. and Townsend et al. presented data that favour biofeedback relative to other procedures, in contrast, Jessup and Neufeld, and Beiman et al. reported evidence that biofeedback was relatively ineffective. While the latter two studies can be criticized for providing insufficient training, the former can be criticized for selecting particularly ineffective treatments with which to compare biofeedback. To date, only Jessup and Neufeld have attempted any sort of placebo control, so further controlled study is necessary before efficacy can be properly resolved.

Finally, there is some recent evidence to suggest that reductions in forehead tension engineered by frontalis EMG feedback do not generalize to other muscle sites, i.e., tension may persist elsewhere in the body even when the frontalis muscle is profoundly relaxed (see Alexander and Smith 1979). If this is the case, it does not bode well for an anxiety treatment based exclusively on forehead tension reduction.

Heart rate biofeedback

Wickramasekera (1974) was again one of the first researchers to apply HR biofeedback to the treatment of anxiety. The patient suffered from cardiac neurosis, i.e. his anxiety attacks were triggered by increases in HR and the conviction that a heart attack was imminent. This persistent fear was disrupting both his home life and his efficiency at work. Treatment consisted of giving the patient biofeedback, initially to both increase and decrease HR. Feedback training then focussed on lowering HR and was conducted when the patient read material associated with increased HR and anxiety. In all, sixteen sessions of treatment were provided, by the end of which the patient was free from anxiety attacks. Benefits in terms of improved relationships at home and greater efficiency at work were also evident. At follow-up, a year after treatment, the patient was still free from anxiety.

Blanchard and Abel (1976) also reported success with HR biofeedback in a single case study. The patient had been raped at the age of ten. As a result, thoughts of rape and sex provoked a dramatic cardiac response: pronounced cardiac acceleration followed by marked deceleration. This generally resulted in the patient blacking out. Following initial baseline HR monitoring with the patient sitting quietly, HR was recorded while the patient listened to tape recorded episodes of rape, which included descriptions of the specific thoughts and events which distressed her. Eight sessions of HR biofeedback were then given to facilitate HR lowering. A further twenty-five feedback sessions were then provided, during which the patient had to attempt to decrease HR while listening to the distressing tape recordings. Sessions without feedback were then introduced. Here the patient was instructed to lower HR while listening to either the previous material or to new, but similarly traumatic recordings. During feedback the patient managed to decrease her HR and to keep it low while listening to the tapes. HR control was still evident with feedback removed. Substantial clinical gains were also evident. The patient reported that she was generally less anxious and that the blackout spells had virtually ceased. At four month follow-up, these gains were maintained.

Gatchel (1977) described a student with an intense fear of enclosed places, i.e. claustrophobia. Again, the patient's anxiety was characterized by a marked cardiac acceleration. Following baseline assessment, biofeedback was provided to facilitate HR slowing. A total of fourteen sessions were undertaken, spread over a period of two months. Gatchel pointed out that, since the feedback training was conducted in a small, enclosed cubicle, the procedure necessitated the practice of HR control in the presence of distressingly claustrophobic circumstances. Nevertheless, the patient managed to lower his HR substantially and, in addition, registered marked clinical improvement. Analysis of daily records of the number and severity of anxiety attacks before, during and after treatment indicated a steady reduction in anxiety.

It is important to note that for all three of these patients, cardiac activity was a central component in their anxiety. Gatchel (1979) has argued that this undoubtedly has an important bearing on outcome, i.e. HR biofeedback is more likely to be effective where HR is a key element in anxiety reactions. Such considerations, however, hardly mitigate the objection that while these data are extremely encouraging, controlled studies are necessary to establish properly the merits of HR biofeedback in this or any other context.

A number of studies attempting some sort of experimental control have now been undertaken. The earliest experiment was reported by Prigatano and Johnson (1972). HR biofeedback was applied with thirteen individuals who displayed an intense fear of spiders. In two sessions, feedback was geared to promote decreases in HR variability. Further feedback sessions were then undertaken while the individuals viewed slides of spiders. A similarly sized control group of spider phobias received false feedback throughout. Following training, both groups were able to approach spiders to a much greater extent than previously. However, there were no group differences; those given false feedback improved just as much as those provided with veridical feedback.

Nunes and Marks (1975) also found no evidence for HR biofeedback in this sort of setting. Their ten patients, all displaying an intense fear of small animals, were gradually exposed to the objects of their fears. HR biofeedback was provided to facilitate reductions in HR in one phase of the study; in the other phase, the *in vivo* exposure procedure was carried out but without the biofeedback provision.

Half the patients started with feedback and proceeded to the no-feedback phase; for the other half, the order of conditions was reversed. Nunes and Marks found that HR was significantly lower during the feedback phase. In addition, all ten patients gained some relief from anxiety. However, the feedback phase was no more effective than the no-feedback phase in this regard. Nunes and Marks concluded that biofeedback added little or nothing to the benefits derived from the gradual *in vivo* exposure technique.

Gatchel et al. (1977) examined the relative merits of HR biofeedback and a conventional relaxation procedure for combating anxieties about public speaking. Gatchel and Proctor (1976) had already reported that HR biofeedback could be of some benefit in this regard. In the earlier study thirty-six college students, identified as extremely fearful of public speaking, were assigned to one of four groups. Groups 1 and 2 received two sessions of biofeedback for HR slowing and in addition, group 1 subjects were given high expectations of success. Groups 3 and 4 performed a tracking task for two sessions, with group 3 also receiving high expectations of success. Group 1 and 2 showed more HR slowing than groups 3 and 4. Further, self-reports of anxiety, as well as observers's evaluations during the delivery of a speech, attested to reliably less anxiety in groups 1 and 2 than in groups 3 and 4. These differences were still evident at four-month follow-up. The manipulation of expectation of success did not seem to affect the outcome significantly.

In the subsequent study (Gatchel et al. 1977), forty students were again allocated to one of four groups. Subjects in group 1 attempted to lower HR with the aid of biofeedback for a total of four sessions. Group 2 subjects practised progressive relaxation, again for four sessions, while group 3 subjects received two sessions of progressive relaxation training and two sessions of HR biofeedback. Subjects in group 4 were given false HR feedback and their final session was specifically designed to convey the impression that HR decreases were being successfully achieved. Anxiety, assessed in the same manner as the previous study, decreased reliably for all four groups following treatment. However, there were no group differences in the extent of improvement. False HR feedback proved just as effective as the other procedures, even though, unlike the others, it occasioned no reduction in actual HR. At follow-up, four to eight weeks after treatment, the clinical picture was much the same. All groups reported benefit, with no group differences being evident.

In a more recent study of public-speaking anxiety, Gatchel et al. (1979) compared the effectiveness of systematic desensitization with two of the previous treatment conditions; the progressive relaxation/HR biofeedback combination and the false HR feedback procedure. The results were much as before. The false feedback group displayed as much reduction in anxiety as the other two groups although, physiologically, it showed less in the way of change. At follow-up, a month after treatment, the subjects were re-evaluated, but in a different public-speaking situation. They had to speak in front of six people on this occasion, instead of the two observers who made up the audience in previous assessments. Anxiety reductions were maintained in all groups but, as before, there were no group differences.

A number of studies of non-anxious individuals might be considered pertinent of the issue of whether HR biofeedback affords an effective means of modifying anxiety and fear reactions. Sirota et al. (1974) provided a group of twenty undergraduate subjects with HR biofeedback during the anticipation of a painful electric shock. For half of the subjects feedback was geared to promote HR slowing, while for the other half, HR acceleration was the desired response. Changes in the appropriate direction were rewarded financially. Subjects were required to rate the aversiveness of the shocks received on a scale of 0–100: the higher the rating, the greater the perceived aversiveness. Differential HR changes were achieved; by the last trial, the increase and decrease groups differed by 11 beats per minute. Ratings of aversiveness also differed between groups; for the HR increase group, the overall average rating was 52.9, while for the decrease group, an average of 38.1 was recorded. Sirota et al. concluded, on the basis of these data, that HR biofeedback might provide a useful general strategy for changing an individual's reactions to anxiety-provoking situations.

In a subsequent study that incorporated a number of improvements in experimental design, Sirota et al. (1976) attempted to replicate these findings. Again, twenty undergraduate students served as subjects. However, in this study, all twenty attempted both HR increase and HR decrease. Ten of the subjects received feedback and bonuses for HR increase in the first phase of the experiment and for HR decrease in the second phase; for the remaining ten, the order of conditions was reversed. Ratings of aversiveness, made as before, showed only a marginal (3.5) difference between conditions in this study. In fact, only for a subgroup, designated as cardiac aware because of their reported awareness of cardiac activity in stressful situations, did the conditions for increasing and decreasing HR occasion reliably different ratings.

Victor et al. (1978) examined much the same phenomena, but used a different stressor: the cold-pressor test. This involves immersing a hand in a bucket of ice-cold water for a set period of time: in this case, 30 seconds. Forty-five subjects were allocated to one of five groups. Following an initial cold-pressor test, subjects in group 1 received twenty-five trials of HR biofeedback plus financial rewards to facilitate HR increase, followed by five trials of attempting HR increase without feedback and reward. Group 2 subjects were treated in the same way, save that HR decrease was the desired response. Group 3 subjects spent the period of the first twenty-five trials reading, and then they attempted to increase HR for five trials without feedback. Group 4 was similar to group 3, save that HR decrease was attempted. Group 5 subjects merely read throughout. Following these different treatments, subjects in all five groups completed a second cold-pressor test. The pain associated with this second immersion was rated on a scale of 1–10, where 1 signified no pain and 10 signified unbearable pain. The average ratings for the five groups in order were: 6.7, 4.0, 6.1, 5.4, 6.3. Statistical analysis revealed that the ratings of groups 1 and 2 differed reliably and that group 2 subjects gave significantly lower ratings of pain than group 5. Victor et al. concluded, like Sirota et al. before them, that biofeedback training could well be useful generally in the management of reactions to stressful stimuli.

However, since none of the studies included a false feedback control condition, it is difficult to judge whether the differences in ratings of aversiveness arose from the actual physiological changes promoted by biofeedback or from the information contained in the biofeedback signal. Several experiments, following from Valins (1966), have now demonstrated that individuals' feelings in a variety of situations can be directed by false HR feedback, irrespective of the actual state of their cardiac functioning. Clearly, the comparison with a false feedback condition is necessary before according veridical HR biofeedback a particular role in the management of stress and anxiety.

Carroll and Evans (1981) have recently included just such a condition. Three groups of ten subjects were exposed to intermittent bursts of loud noise. Two of the groups attempted HR control before the noise bursts, one with the aid of HR biofeedback and one without. On half of the trials, HR increase was the desired response; on the other half, HR decrease was attempted. The third group did not attempt HR control, but instead received false feedback that their HRs were either increasing or decreasing before the noise bursts. The aversiveness of the noise bursts was rated on two 21-point scales, one of unpleasantness and one of loudness; higher ratings indicated greater unpleasantness and loudness. Only the veridical biofeedback group demonstrated reliably different HR changes during attempted HR increase and decrease. The HRs of the false-feedback subjects were unaffected by the direction of the change signalled by the biofeedback display. However, a significant differential effect on subjects' ratings of the noise bursts, in terms of loudness and pleasantness, was apparent only for the false-feedback group. The lack of effect for veridical feedback in this study can perhaps be attributed to the somewhat modest differential effects in the HR increase and decrease conditions; a difference of only 6 beats per minute was observed in the present study. Victor et al. observed an average difference of more than 10 beats per minute and Sirota et al. (1974), as indicated, reported a difference that reached 11 beats per minute. In contrast, Sirota et al.'s (1976) subjects managed a difference of only 7 beats per minute between increase and decrease attempts. Thus differences in ratings of aversiveness are obtained only where there are substantial HR effects. Given Carroll and Evans' results for false feedback, it might be argued that training in HR control affects subjects' assessments of stressful stimulation only in as far as the biofeedback signal indicates discriminably distinct HR levels in the different conditions. Thus, it is the nature of the feedback message rather than the HR change *per se* that influences stimulus ratings. While further study is undoubtedly required before definite conclusions can be drawn, these studies can hardly be regarded as offering unambiguous support for biofeedback in the management of anxiety and stress.

Taken together, the evidence for HR biofeedback in the context of fear and anxiety is far from compelling. Although the early single case studies report favourable outcomes, remarkably few patients were involved. Further, the results of more recent, controlled investigations are unsupportive. Gatchel's research consistently indicates that veridical HR biofeedback is no more effective than false feedback. The experiments conducted on non-anxious subjects tell much the same sort of story; false feedback would seem to be just as effective.

Finally, there is evidence to suggest that individuals reporting anxiety are particularly bad at controlling HR (for a detailed review see Carroll 1979). Blankstein and Egner (1974) assigned their subjects to high- medium- and low-anxiety groups on the basis of their answers to a standard questionnaire measuring anxiety. Biofeedback was then provided as subjects attempted HR control. The low anxiety subjects were distinctly better at both increasing and decreasing HR. This effect appeared early in training and increased in a final session during which no feedback was provided. Similarly, Stephens et al. (1975) observed that the extent of HR control on days 3, 4 and 5 of a five-day training schedule was reliably related to anxiety as measured by the questionnaire. Again, subjects low in anxiety demonstrated the best cardiac control and again their superiority held for both acceleratory and deceleratory control. More recently, Cox and McGuiness (1977) reported that subjects who scored high on an anxiety questionnaire were unable to lower their HRs reliably with biofeedback; only subjects selected as low on anxiety managed to decrease HR substantially. However, high anxiety subjects were, in this study, able to increase their HRs successfully. Considered together, these studies offer little support for the use of HR biofeedback in the treatment of anxiety. Individuals identified as anxious by questionnaires are uniformly observed to be relatively bad at decreasing HR.

Conclusions

Little consistent evidence can be mustered in favour of the application of biofeedback, either of HR or EMG, in this context. Although data from the early uncontrolled case studies look promising, such data will always be insufficient to establish efficacy. As emphasized elsewhere, controlled experiments are necessary. However, the controlled experiments that have been conducted to date, can hardly be regarded as providing much in the way of compelling support for biofeedback. In general, biofeedback offers no advantage over simpler therapeutic alternatives and is no more effective than false feedback. In the case of EMG feedback, two studies do indicate some advantage for feedback relative to other treatments. However, it is likely that much of this reflects the selection of particularly ineffective alternatives against which to compare feedback. HR biofeedback is without even this sort of support. It is difficult to avoid the conclusion that in most instances HR biofeedback represents an elaborate and rather expensive placebo. Nevertheless, it remains possible, as Gatchel (1979) has proposed, that HR feedback may be of some direct relevance in cases where HR acceleration is a central component of the anxiety reaction. However, proposals such as this must ultimately rest on the outcome of controlled study.

Finally, in the case of EMG feedback, there is evidence to suggest that reductions in frontalis muscle tension, the focus of studies to date, are not necessarily parallelled by reductions in tension elsewhere in the body. With regard to HR control, it would appear that individuals exhibiting high levels of anxiety are relatively unsuccessful at decreasing HR. Both of these results cast further doubt on the appropriateness of both frontalis EMG and HR biofeedback as treatments for fear and anxiety.

Chapter 9

Conclusions

Introduction

Over the past 15 years or so, biofeedback has been applied to a wide variety of clinical disorders; new applications continue to be advanced. The present text inevitably has had to be selective, as a completely comprehensive evaluation of biofeedback would need several volumes.

Judging the efficacy of any treatment is rarely a simple matter. However, the problems encountered are very much aggravated where few systematic data are available. Consequently, applications which have as yet attracted only limited study have been excluded from consideration; instead attention has focused on the most fully researched uses. Consideration of these, it was presumed, should provide surer estimations of effectiveness.

While a selection criterion of this sort has meant sacrificing some breadth, it was intended that nothing be lost in the way of depth and the applications chosen for inclusion be examined rigorously. It is worth stressing that the burden of proof for any new therapy invariably lies with its proponents and some of the conditions that must be satisfied are summarized in the introductory chapter. Suffice to say that casual and unsystematic observations of clinical improvement offer insufficient surety; improvements need to be confirmed in the context of adequately controlled research.

Some might regard such conditions as unduly strict: as unnecessary obstacles in the path of patients seeking treatment and therapists striving to provide it. However, the barely discarded practices of purging and blood-letting should caution us against abandoning science for expediency. Not only do patients have a right to treatment, as many insist, but they also have a right to the right treatment. Only by insisting on careful and controlled study, can we assure effective treatment for a particular condition, and only by observing the rules of science can the public be protected from inappropriate and bogus remedies.

Finally, while the optimal targets for biofeedback may prove to lie elsewhere, the applications selected for scrutiny in the present text are those which at first sight seemed most likely to yield dividends. What, then, does our examination of biofeedback in practice reveal?

Biofeedback in practice

Little consistent support could be found for the application of blood pressure biofeedback to essential hypertension. So many of the early studies are characterized by poor methodology; inadequate baseline assessment, absent or insufficient follow-up, and lack of control conditions or treatments are common weaknesses. It is difficult to attach much weight to positive outcomes in such circumstances. More telling, perhaps, is the revelation that as methodology has improved, so in general, the indications for biofeedback have diminished. The later controlled studies are almost uniformly unfavourable; biofeedback would seem to offer no advantage over much more simply administered relaxation techniques. Overall, the most encouraging data are those presented by Kristt and Engel (1975) and Patel (1975). However, they hardly constitute a compelling case for biofeedback. Patel's studies employed skin resistance feedback anyway and supplemented this with a series of yoga-based techniques.

It is quite likely, given Datey et al.'s (1969) favourable results with a yoga exercise *per se*, that yoga rather than biofeedback constituted the active ingredient. It is also difficult to determine unequivocably the effective element in Kristt and Engels' single group study. For example, the regular monitoring of blood pressure at home by their patients was undoubtedly a salutary experience.

The use of HR biofeedback for the correction of cardiac arrhythmias has yet to receive controlled examination. Although the data available are encouraging, they are derived entirely from single and multiple case studies. As such, they can hardly be regarded as final proof. While a range of severe cardiac irregularities have improved with treatment, it is impossible at this stage to say whether or not HR biofeedback was critical to that improvement. Laboratory studies have now demonstrated that HR control, both acceleratory and deceleratory, can be managed without the aid of feedback. In fact, there is some uncertainty as to whether HR biofeedback offers much advantage over instructions alone. Accordingly, biofeedback might not have been essential to the HR adjustments achieved by these patients.

While biofeedback may yet prove of value in the context of cardiac arrthymias, there is little to commend the use of biofeedback for Raynaud's disease. Here, even the early case studies offer only the most marginal support; only a fraction of the patients treated seem to have gained lasting benefit. In addition, it is not at all clear that biofeedback was the primary source of improvement in the few successful cases. Details provided by Schwartz (1973), for example, strongly imply that factors other than biofeedback were the effective agents for his successful patient. Schwartz's feedback training procedure included the presentation of slides as rewards for appropriate vascular changes. This particular patient, a practising psychoanalyst, was given to free association and used the slides as stimuli for his mental excursions. Evidently, in one of the later sessions the slide projector stuck, bathing the screen in bright light. This stimulated images in the patient of the sun, warmth, beaches and so on, which in turn proved particularly helpful in warming his feet and offered a strategy for effecting relief outside the laboratory. According to Schwartz, if the patient's feet became cold, whatever the circumstances, all he had to do was revive these images and he would gain relief. Thus, it would seem to be those autogenic-type images, inadvertently stimulated by a procedural accident, and not the biofeedback *per se*, that accounted for the patient's sustained improvement. Such an interpretation accords well with the results of the one controlled study conducted so far. Surwit et al. (1978) in a study involving large numbers of Raynaud's disease sufferers, found that biofeedback added nothing to the gains produced by autogenic exercises alone.

The application of biofeedback of hand temperature or differential hand-forehead temperature for the treatment of migraine is also poorly indicated. Favourable evidence from uncontrolled studies, given their intrinsic limitations, must be regarded as less than definitive. In addition, most of the uncontrolled explorations employed complex treatment packages of which biofeedback was one of many elements. Inevitably in such circumstances, it remains possible that any observed clinical gains resulted from one or other of the adjunctive treatments: for example, relaxation or autogenic training, since these appear to be reasonably effective in other contexts. The results of the few controlled studies provide clear confirmation that reservations of this sort are more than justified. While there is some evidence that temperature biofeedback is more effective than no treatment at all, although even this is not wholly without counterindications (see Kewman and Roberts 1980), it would seem to offer no advantage over simpler and less costly alternatives. Further, studies by Mullinix et al. (1978) and Kewman and Roberts (1980) raise serious doubts about whether biofeedback in this context has any specific therapeutic effects whatsoever.

Mullinix et al. observed that while patients provided with veridical temperature feedback displayed greater increases in temperature than patients given false feedback, veridical feedback afforded no therapeutic advantage. Similarly, Kewman and Roberts found that feedback for hand-warming was no more effective for migraine than feedback for hand-cooling, even though there were reliable differences in hand temperature between the two groups of patients. These results are consistent with the view that any clinical gains from treatment with biofeedback are largely attributable to non-specific, placebo factors. Finally, feedback of forehead blood flow has, as yet, received only minimal study, but data from the one controlled investigation provide few grounds for optimism. Cohen et al. (1980) found that this mode of treatment was no more effective than differential temperature feedback, or alpha or EMG feedback for that matter. The equivalence of feedback modality here once more reinforces the impression that those who benefit do so through fairly non-specific agencies and not as a result of any specific biofeedback effect.

In contrast to the indications for temperature biofeedback and migraine, data from tension headache studies, comparing veridical and non-veridical EMG feedback, make it hard to discount the successful outcomes described in uncontrolled case reports as placebo effects. Biofeedback geared to reduce frontalis muscle tension has been observed to alleviate both the incidence and severity of tension headaches reliably more than analogous but false feedback. However, Cram's (1980) and Carrobles et al.'s (1981) findings are difficult to explain without recourse to some sort of placebo mechanism. Although coventional EMG biofeedback, according to Cram, benefited patients more than false feedback, it offered no advantage over feedback designed to stabilize forehead muscle tension at a high level, despite the fact that this particular contingency successfully sustained relatively high levels of tension. A significant proportion of Carrobles et al's patients improved sufficiently during baseline assessment to render treatment unnecessary. Further, although EMG biofeedback does appear to produce better results than false feedback or no specific treatment, studies comparing feedback with therapeutic alternatives reveal that it is no more effective in the long run than simple relaxation procedures. Given equivalent efficacy, considerations of cost and ease of administration would argue for relaxation training, and against biofeedback, as the preferred treatment for tension headache.

The application of EMG feedback to neuromuscular disorders would seem a much better prospect. A substantial number of patients, suffering from a range of severely disabling conditions, seem to have derived benefit as a result of treatment with biofeedback. However, even here, it is necessary to exercise caution. Since the data have emerged primarily from uncontrolled case studies, unqualified assertions of efficacy would still seem to be premature. Clinical improvement might reflect mainly the placebo of a new and technologically impressive therapy. So far, only one study (Lee et al. 1976) has broached the placebo issue and it contained too many weaknesses to afford a satisfactory answer. In addition, while many of the patients treated with EMG feedback are reported to have responded minimally or not at all to previous therapeutic efforts, the relative merits of biofeedback and more traditional modes of treatment have rarely been compared directly. Further, the studies reported by Basmajian et al. (1975) and Mroczek et al. (1978), which did attempt such a comparison, are only marginally favourable to biofeedback. In the former, an advantage for biofeedback was apparent in only one of the two major outcome measures, and in the latter, biofeedback actually yielded no better results, although it was more economical in terms of patient-therapist contact. Clearly, additional controlled study is essential. Without it, the status of EMG biofeedback in neuromuscular rehabilitation must remain somewhat uncertain: a promising, but not, as yet, fully established treatment.

While a lack of relevant data prohibits us from

discounting placebo and expectancy as possible sources of relief in the area of EMG feedback and neuromuscular rehabilitation, the actual evidence available for EEG feedback suggests that the clinical gains experienced by epileptic patients owe much to non-specific agencies of this sort. First of all, although a fair number of epileptics have experienced some measure of improvement with EEG biofeedback, outcome does not seem to depend on the precise focus of the feedback facility; reductions in seizure activity seem to be quite independent of the target frequency used and no particular frequency band is more effective than any other. Second, whatever the frequency selected for feedback, therapeutic outcome and voluntary EEG control correlate poorly; clinical improvement has been noted in the absence of EEG control, and EEG control has been demonstrated without commensurate improvements in seizure activity. Third the introduction of bogus EEG feedback has, in general, failed to disrupt therapeutic gains. Although Kuhlman and Allison (1977) reported that an initial bout of false feedback produced no improvement in epileptic condition, it is possible that the exposure to false feedback was too brief and that a longer trial would have brought benefits. Considered as a whole, the evidence to date suggests that some non-specific, possibly placebo, influence is at work here. It should be stressed that there is nothing inherently wrong with a treatment which achieves its ends in this way. In fact there is much sense to the notion that we should make more concerted efforts to understand placebo effects and to harness them more effectively for therapeutic advantage. Nevertheless, if EEG biofeedback is primarily a placebo, it must be possible to devise a less elaborate, less expensive and less time-consuming one.

Both EMG and HR biofeedback have been used to treat debilitating fears and anxiety. Neither feedback modality has received overwhelming support. While the early uncontrolled studies provide some encouragement, subsequent controlled research paints a decidedly less rosy picture as frequently seems to be the case. Of the two, EMG feedback can muster somewhat better support than HR feedback. Two of the controlled studies reviewed (Canter et al, 1975; Townsend et al. 1975) indicated some advantage for EMG biofeedback relative to other treatments. However as pointed out previously, these studies are open to the criticism that relatively ineffective alternatives were chosen for comparison with biofeedback. In addition, patients receiving EMG feedback in the Townsend et al. study also practised progressive relaxation. Consequently, it is impossible to determine which of these two components of the treatment package inspired the relatively high level of clinical improvement. Further, in sharp contrast to these indications of relative efficacy, Jessup and Neufeld (1977) and Beiman et al. (1978) found that EMG biofeedback was no more effective than a range of simple relaxation techniques, although it might be contended that there was insufficient feedback training in both studies to afford a definitive test of relative efficacy. Finally, evidence is accumulating that decreases in frontalis muscle tension, the focus of studies to date, do not necessarily imply reduced tension elsewhere in the body. Overall, then, the available data regarding EMG feedback as a treatment for fear and anxiety are ambiguous; additional controlled study is clearly necessary to resolve matters one way or the other. In the case of HR biofeedback, the results of the controlled studies conducted so far are much more consistent. Generally, HR feedback is observed to offer no advantage over simpler therapeutic alternatives and to be no more effective than false feedback. In addition, given that individuals who exhibit high levels of anxiety would seem to be particularly poor at cardiac control, the outlook for HR biofeedback in this context must be regarded as exceedingly bleak.

Conclusion

At the outset, the possibilities seemed limitless. Certainly, biofeedback's proponents were far from reticent in proclaiming its potential (see, for example, Brown 1974 and Karlins and Andrews 1972). Promotional pieces in the popular press as well as articles in traditionally more sober academic outlets all testified to the possible benefits. While the latter were usually, although not invariably, more cautious in their pronouncements, the difference was only of degree not sentiment. Occasionally, an almost evangelical passion could be detected amid the conditional verbs and qualifying phrases that characterize academic modes of expression. By simply extending our capacities for self-control into areas generally resistant to conscious regulation, biofeedback would provide us with a unique means of regulating health and combating disease – or so it was argued.

Expectations ran high in the early days; much was promised. Has that promise been fufilled? A cold, hard look fifteen years on would indicate that it has not. In most of the areas of application, biofeedback is poorly indicated. Either its effects are variable and/or short-lived, or they are no greater than those produced by simpler, less expensive alternatives, or they can be attributed to the agency of expectancy and placebo. Even in the few areas where the balance of present evidence appears more flattering, such as cardiac arrhythmias and neuromuscular disorders, a large measure of uncertainty remains. Experience with other applications of biofeedback should caution us against placing too much reliance on data, however favourable, generated almost entirely by uncontrolled case studies. Typically, positive indications from case studies have not been substantiated by the results of more rigorously controlled research.

It is difficult to avoid the conclusion that biofeedback has been, on the whole, a rather unproductive venture. In fact, rarely has so much been expected and so little delivered. Admittedly, several of the controlled studies that indicate little or no advantage for biofeedback relative to simpler therapeutic alternatives or false feedback are open to the criticism that they provided insufficient training to allow biofeedback a fair trial. Certainly, many of the early case studies can claim to be more rigorous in this respect than some of the later controlled experiments. Clearly, the results of controlled research are much more compelling when relatively extensive training has been undertaken. In addition, as was pointed out earlier, a therapist's enthusiasm for a particular procedure is undoubtedly not without significance for therapeutic outcome. However, this cuts both ways. Not only might over-optimism compensate for an intrinsically ineffective treatment, but scepticism might equally detract from a potentially effective one. It is possible that some of the researchers undertaking controlled studies had somewhat low expectations for biofeedback. Such reservations and speculations aside, it is apparent that, in its major areas of application, biofeedback at present just does not command the sort of empirical evidence necessary to establish it as the treatment of choice. While evidence may be forthcoming in some areas, only a minority of applications would seem to justify such optimism. It is a far cry from the early promises of a new and radical panacea.

References

Adler, C. and Adler, S. (1976) Biofeedback-psychotherapy for the treatment of headaches: A five year clinical follow-up, *Headache*, **16**, 189–91.

Alexander, A. B. and Smith, D. D. (1979) Clinical applications of EMG biofeedback, in R. J. Gatchel and K. P. Price (eds) *Clinical applications of biofeedback: Appraisal and status*, Pergamon Press, Oxford and New York.

Andrews, J. M. (1964) Neuromuscular re-education of the hemiplegic with the aid of the electromyogram, *Archives of Physical Medicine and Rehabilitation*, **45**, 530–2.

Andreychuk, T. and Skriver, C. (1975) Hypnosis and biofeedback in the treatment of migraine headache, *International Journal of Clinical and Experimental Hypnosis*, **23**, 172–83.

Basmajian, J. V., Kukulka, C. G., Narayan, M. G. and Takebe, K. (1975) Biofeedback treatment of foot-drop after stroke compared with standard rehabilitation technique: Effects on voluntary control and strength, *Archives of Physical Medicine and Rehabilitation*, **56**, 231–6.

Beecher, H. L. (1961) Surgery as placebo: A quantitative study of bias. *Journal of the American Medical Association*, **176**, 1102–7.

Beiman, I., Israel, E. and Johnson, S. A. (1978) During training and post training effects of live and taped extended progressive relaxation, self-relaxation, and electromyogram biofeedback, *Journal of Consulting and Clinical Psychology*, **46**, 314–21.

Benson, H. (1975) *The relaxation response*, William Morrow, New York.

Benson, H., Shapiro, D., Tursky, B. and Schwartz, G. E. (1971) Decreased systolic blood pressure through operant conditioning techniques in patients with essential hypertension, *Science*, **173**, 740–2.

Bild, R. and Adams, H. E. (1980) Modification of migraine headaches by cephalic blood volume pulse and EMG biofeedback, *Journal of Consulting and Clinical Psychology*, **48**, 51–7.

Blanchard, E. B. (1979) Biofeedback and the modification of cardiovascular dysfunctions, in R. J. Gatchel and K. P. Price (eds), *Clinical applications of biofeedback: Appraisal and status*, Pergamon Press, Oxford and New York.

Blanchard, E. B. and Abel, G. G. (1976) An experimental case study of the biofeedback treatment of a rape-induced psychological cardiovascular disorder, *Behavior Therapy*, **7**, 113–19.

Blanchard, E. B. and Haynes, M. R. (1975) Biofeedback treatment of a case of Raynaud's disease, *Journal of Behavior Therapy and Experimental Psychiatry*, **6**, 230–4.

Blanchard, E. B., Miller, S. T., Abel, G. G., Haynes, M. R. and Wicker, R. (1977) The failure of blood pressure feedback in treating hypertension. Unpublished manuscript. (Details in Blanchard, E. B. (1979) Biofeedback and the modification of cardiovascular dysfunctions.) in R. J. Gatchel and K. P. Price (eds), *Clinical applications of biofeedback: Appraisal and status*, Pergamon Press, Oxford and New York.

Blanchard, E. B., Theobald, D. E. Williamson, D. A., Silver, B. V. amd Brown, D. A. (1978) Temperature feedback in the treatment of migraine headaches, *Archives of General Psychiatry*, **35**, 581–8.

Blanchard, E. B. and Young, L. D. (1973) Self-control of cardiac functioning: A promise as yet unfulfilled, *Psychological Bulletin*, **79**, 145–63.

Blanchard, E. B., Young L. D. and Haynes, M. R. (1975) A simple feedback system for the treatment of elevated blood pressure, *Behavior Therapy*, **6**, 241–5.

Blankstein, K. R. and Egner, K. (1974) Effects of trait anxiety on voluntary heart rate control and subjective tenseness, *Psychophysiology*, **11**, 241–2.

Booker, H. E., Rubow, R. T. and Coleman, P. J. (1969) Simplified feedback in neuromuscular retraining: An automated approach using electromyographic signals, *Archives of Physical Medicine and Rehabilitation*, **50**, 621–5.

Brener, J. and Kleinman, R. A. (1970) Learned control of decreases in systolic blood pressure, *Nature*, **226**, 1063–4.

Brown, B. B. (1974) *New mind, new body*, Hodder & Stoughton, London.

Brudny, J., Korein, J., Grynbaum, B. B., Friedmann, L. W., Weinstein, S., Sachs-Frankel, G. and Belandres, P. V. (1976) EMG feedback therapy: Review of treatment of 114 patients, *Archives of Physical Medicine and Rehabilitation*, **57**, 55–61.

Budzynski, T. and Stoyva, J. (1973) Biofeedback techniques in behavior therapy, in D. Shapiro, T. X. Barber, L. V. DiCara, J. Kamiya, N. E. Miller, and J. Stoyva (eds), *Biofeedback and self-control*, Aldine, Chicago.

Budzynski, T., Stoyva, J. and Adler, C. (1970) Feedback-induced muscle relaxation: Application to tension headache, *Journal of Behavior Therapy and Experimental Psychiatry*, **1**, 205–1.

Budzynski, T. H., Stoyva, J. M., Adler, C. S. and Mullaney, D. J. (1973) EMG biofeedback and tension headache: A controlled outcome study, *Psychosomatic Medicine*, **35**, 484–96.

Cabral, R J. and Scott, D. F. (1976) Effects of two desensitization techniques, biofeedback and relaxation, on intractable epilepsy: Follow-up study, *Journal of Neurology, Neurosurgery and Psychiatry*, **39**, 504–7.

Canter, A., Kondo, C. Y. and Knott, J. R. (1975) A comparison of EMG feedback and progressive muscle relaxation training in anxiety neurosis, *British Journal of Psychiatry*, **127**, 470–7.

Carrobles, J. A. I., Cardona, A. and Santacreu, J. (1981) Shaping and generalization procedures in the EMG-biofeedback treatment of tension headaches, *British Journal of Clinical Psychology*, **20**, 49–56.

Carroll, D. (1979) Voluntary heart rate control: The role of individual differences, *Biological Psychology*, **8**, 137–57.

Carroll, D. and Evans, L. (1981) Effects of heart-rate biofeedback and false feedback on reactions to stressful stimulation, *Perceptual and Motor Skills*, **53**, 387–93.

Chesney, M. A. and Shelton, J. L. (1976) A comparison of muscle relaxation and electromyogram biofeedback treatments for muscle contraction headache, *Journal of Behavior Therapy and Experimental Psychiatry*, **7**, 221–5.

Cleeland, C. S. (1973) Behavioral techniques in the modification of spasmodic torticollis, *Neurology*, **23**, 1241–7.

Cohen, M. J., McArthur, D. L. and Rickles, W. H. (1980) Comparison of four biofeedback treatments for migraine headaches: Physiologic and headache variables, *Psychosomatic Medicine*, **42**, 463–80.

Cott, A., Pavloski, R. P. and Black, A. H. (1979) Reducing epileptic seizures through operant conditioning of central nervous system activity: Procedural variables, *Science*, **203**, 73–5.

Cox, D. J., Freundlich, A. and Meyer, R. G. (1975) Differential effectiveness of electromyographic feedback, verbal relaxation instructions, and medication placebo with tension headaches, *Journal of Consulting and Clinical Psychology*, **43**, 892–9.

Cox, R. J. and McGuiness, D. (1977) The effect of chronic anxiety level upon self-control of heart rate, *Biological Psychology*, **5**, 7–14.

Cram, J. R. (1980) EMG biofeedback and the treatment of tension headaches: A systematic analysis of treatment components, *Behavior Therapy*, **11**, 699–710.

Datey, K. K., Deshmukh, S. N., Dalvi, C. P. and Vinekar, S. L. (1969) 'Shavasan': A yogic exercise in the management of hypertension, *Angiology*, **20**, 325–33.

Elder, S. T., Ruiz, Z. R., Deabler, H. S. and Dillenkoffer, R. L. (1973) Instrumental conditioning of diastolic blood pressure in essential hypertensive patients, *Journal of Applied Behavior Analysis*, **6**, 377–82.

Elder, S. T. and Eustis, N. K. (1975) Instrumental blood pressure conditioning in outpatient hypertensives, *Behaviour Research & Therapy*, **13**, 185–8.

Engel, B. T. and Bleecker, E. R. (1974) Application of operant conditioning techniques to the control of cardiac arrhythmias, in P. A. Obrist, A. H. Black, J. Brener and L. V. DiCara (eds), *Cardiovascular psychophysiology*, Aldine, Chicago.

Epstein, L. H., Hersen, M. and Hemphill, P. D. (1974) Music feedback in the treatment of tension headache: An experimental case study, *Journal of Behavior Therapy and Experimental Psychiatry*, **5**, 59–63.

Epstein, L, H. and Abel, G. G. (1977) An analysis of biofeedback training effects for tension headache patients, *Behavior Therapy*, **8**, 37–47.

Finley, W. W. (1974) Reduction of seizures and normalization of the EEG in a severe epileptic following sensorimotor biofeedback training, in N. E. Miller, T. X. Barker, L. V.

DiCara, J. Kamiya, D. Shapiro and J. Stoyva (eds), *Biofeedback and self-control*, Aldine, Chicago.

Finley, W. W. (1976) Effects of sham feedback following successful SMR training in an epileptic: Follow-up study, *Biofeedback and Self-regulation*, **1**, 227–35.

Finley, W. W. (1977) Operant conditioning of the EEG in two patients with epilepsy: Methodologic and clinical considerations, *Pavlovian Journal of Biological Science*, **12**, 93–111.

Finley, W. W., Niman, C. A., Standley, J. and Ender, P. (1976) Frontal EMG-biofeedback training of athetoid cerebral palsy patients: A report of six cases, *Biofeedback and Self-regulation*, **1**, 169–82.

Finley, W. W., Niman, C. A., Standley, J. and Wansley, R. A. (1977) Electrophysiologic behavior modification of frontal EMG in cerebral-palsied children, *Biofeedback and Self-regulation*, **2**, 59–79.

Fish, D., Mayer, N. and Herman, R. (1976) Biofeedback (letter), *Archives of Physical Medicine and Rehabilitation*, **57**, 152.

Friar, L. R. and Beatty, J. (1976) Migraine: Management by trained control of vasoconstriction, *Journal of Consulting and Clinical Psychology*, **44**,, 46–53.

Fried, F., Lamberti, J. and Sneed, P. (1977) Treatment of tension and migraine headaches with biofeedback techniques, *Missouri Medicine*, **74**, 253–5.

Friedman, A. P., von Storch, T. J. C. and Merritt, H. H. (1954) Migraine and tension headaches: A clinical study of two thousand cases, *Neurology*, **4**, 773–88.

Friedman, H. and Taub, H. A. (1977) The use of hypnosis and biofeedback procedures for essential hypertension, *International Journal of Clinical and Experimental Hypnosis*, **25**, 335–47.

Friedman, H. and Taub, H. A. (1978) A six-month follow-up of the use of hypnosis and biofeedback procedures in essential hypertension, *American Journal of Clinical Hypnosis*, **20**, 184–8.

Gastaut, H. (1952) Étude electrocorticographique de la reactivité des rhythmes rolandiques, *Revue Neurologique*, **87**, 176–82.

Gatchel, R. J. (1977) Therapeutic effectiveness of voluntary heart rate control in reducing anxiety, *Journal of Consulting and Clinical Psychology*, **45**, 689–91.

Gatchel, R. J. (1979) Biofeedback and the treatment of fear and anxiety, in R. J. Gatchel and K. P. Price (eds), *Clinical applications of biofeedback: Appraisal and status*, Pergamon Press, Oxford and New York.

Gatchel, R. J., Hatch, J. P., Maynard, A., Turns, R. and Taunton–Blackwood, A. (1979) Comparative effectiveness of heart rate biofeedback, false-feedback and systematic desensitization in reducing speech anxiety: Short-term and long-term effectiveness, *Journal of Consulting and Clinical Psychology*, **47**, 620–2.

Gatchel, R. J. and Proctor, J. D. (1976) Effectiveness of voluntary heart rate control in reducing speech anxiety, *Journal of Consulting and Clinical Psychology*, **44**, 381–98.

Gatchel, R. J., Hatch, J. P., Watson, P. J., Smith, D. and Gaas, E. (1977) Comparative effectiveness of voluntary heart rate control and muscular relaxation as active coping skills for reducing speech anxiety, *Journal of Consulting and Clinical Psychology*, **45**, 1093–100.

Goldman, H., Kleinman, K. M., Snow, M. Y., Bidus, D. R. and Korol, B. (1975) Relationship between essential hypertension and cognitive functioning: Effects of biofeedback, *Psychophysiology*, **12**, 569–73.

Harris, F. A., Spelman, F. A. and Hymer, J. W. (1974) Electronic sensory aids as treatment for cerebral-palsied children. Inapproprioception: Part 2, *Physical Therapy*, **54**, 354–65.

Hart, J. D. and Cichanski, K. A. (1981) A comparison of frontal and neck EMG biofeedback in the treatment of muscle-contraction headache, *Biofeedback and Self-regulation*, **6**, 63–74.

Haynes, S. N., Griffin, P., Mooney, D. and Parise, M. (1975) Electromyographic biofeedback and relaxation instructions in the treatment of muscle contraction headaches, *Behavior Therapy*, **6**, 672–8.

Hutchings, D. and Reinking, R. H. (1976) Tension headaches: What form of therapy is most effective? *Biofeedback and Self-regulation*, **1**, 183–90.

Jacobson, A. M., Hackett, T. P., Surman, O. S. and Silverberg, E. (1973) Raynaud phenomenon: Treatment with hypnotic and operant technique, *Journal of the American Medical Association*, **225**, 739–40.

Jankel, W. R. (1978) Bells Palsy: Muscle re-education by electromyograph feedback, *Archives of Physical Medicine and Rehabilitation*, **59**, 240–2.

Jessup, B. A. and Neufeld, R. W. J. (1977) Effects of biofeedback and 'autogenic relaxation' techniques on physiological and subjective responses in psychiatric patients: A preliminary analysis, *Behavior Therapy*, **8**, 160–7.

Johnson, H. E. and Garton, W. H. (1973) Muscle re-education in hemiplegia by the use of an electromyographic device, *Archives of Physical Medicine and Rehabilitation*, **54**, 320–5.

Johnson, R. K. and Meyer, R. G. (1974) Phased biofeedback approach for epileptic seizure control, *Journal of Behavior Therapy and Experimental Psychiatry*, **5**, 185–7.

Johnson, W. G. and Turin, A. (1975) Biofeedback treatment of migraine headache: A systematic case study, *Behavior Therapy*, **6**, 394–7.

Kamiya, J. (1968) Conscious control of brain waves, *Psychology Today*, **1**, 57–60.

Kannel, W. B. (1977) Importance of hypertension as a major risk factor in cardiovascular disease, in J. Genest, E. Koiw and O. Kuchel (eds), *Hypertension physiopathology and treatment*, McGraw–Hill, New York.

Kaplan, B. J. (1975) Biofeedback in epileptics: Equivocal relationship of reinforced EEG frequency to seizure reduction, *Epilepsia*, **16**, 477–85.

Karlins, M. and Andrews, L. M. (1972) *Biofeedback: Turning on the power of your mind*, Warner Books, New York.

Kentsmith, D., Strider, F., Copenhaver, J. and Jacques, D. (1976) Effects of biofeedback upon the suppression of migraine symptoms and plasma dopamine-B-hydroxylase activity, *Headache*, **16**, 173–7.

Kewman, D. and Roberts, A. H. (1980) Skin temperature biofeedback and migraine headaches: A double blind study, *Biofeedback and Self-regulation*, **5**, 327–46.

King, J. T. (1920) An instance of voluntary acceleration of the pulse, *Johns Hopkins Bulletin*, **27**, 303–5.

Kleinman, K. M., Goldman, H., Snow, M. Y. and Korol, B. (1977) Relationship between essential hypertension and cognitive functioning II: Effects of biofeedback training generalized to non-laboratory environment, *Psychophysiology*, **14**, 192–7.

Kondo, C. and Canter, A. (1977) True and false electromyographic feedback: Effect on tension headache, *Journal of Abnormal Psychology*, **86**, 93–5.

Kristt, D. A. and Engel, B. T. (1975) Learned control of blood pressure in patients with high blood pressure, *Circulation*, **51**, 370–8.

Kuhlman, W. W. (1978) Functional topography of the human mu rhythm, *Electroencephalography and Clinical Neurophysiology*, **45**, 290–4.

Kuhlman, W. N. and Allison, T. (1977) EEG feedback training in the treatment of epilepsy: Some questions and answers, *Pavlovian Journal of Biological Science*, **12**, 112–22.

Kuhlman, W. N. and Kaplan, B. J. (1979) Clinical application of EEG feedback training, in R. J. Gatchel and K. P. Price (eds), *Clinical applications of biofeedback: Appraisal and status*, Pergamon Press, Oxford and New York.

Kukulka, C. G., Brown, D. M. and Basmajian, J. V. (1975) Biofeedback training for early finger joint mobilization, *American Journal of Occupational Therapy*, **29**, 469–70.

Lee, K., Hill, E., Johnston, R. and Smiehorowski, T. (1976) Myofeedback for muscle retraining in hemiplegic patients, *Archives of Physical Medicine and Rehabilitation*, **57**, 588–91.

Lown, B., Temple, J. V., Reich, P., Ganghan, C., Regestein, Q. and Hai, H. (1976) Basis for recurring ventricular fibrillation in the absence of coronary heart disease and its management, *New England Journal of Medicine*, **294**, 623–9.

Lubar, J. F. (1977) Electroencephalographic biofeedback methodology and the management of epilepsy, *Pavlovian Journal of Biological Science*, **12**, 147–85.

Lubar, J. F. and Bahler, W. W. (1976) Behavioral management of epileptic seizures following EEG biofeedback training of sensorimotor rhythms, *Biofeedback and Self-regulation*, **1**, 77–104.

Luborsky, L., Crits–Cristeph, P., Brady, J. P., Kron, R. E., Weiss, T., Cohen, M. and Levy, L. (1982) Behavioral vs. pharmacological treatment for essential hypertension: A needed comparison, *Psychosomatic medicine*, **44**, 203–13.

Luria, A. R. (1958) *The mind of a mnemonist*, Basic Books, New York.

Mandler, G. (1975) *Mind and emotion*, Wiley, New York.

Martin, P. R. and Mathews, A. M. (1978) Tension headaches: Psychophysiological investigation and treatment, *Journal of Psychosomatic Research*, **22**, 389–99.

Marinacci, A. A. and Horande, M. (1960) Electromyogram in neuromuscular re-education, *Bulletin of the Los Angeles Neurological Society*, **25**, 57–71.

Medina, J. L., Diamond, S. and Franklin, M. A. (1976) Biofeedback therapy for migraine, *Headache*, **16**, 115–8.

Miller, N. E. (1972) Postscript, in D. Singh & C. T. Morgan (eds) *Current status of physiological psychology: Readings*, Brooks–Cole, Monterey, California.

Miller, N. E. (1975) Clinical applications of biofeedback: Voluntary control of heart rate, rhythm, and blood pressure, in H. I. Russek (ed), *New horizons in cardiovascular practice*, University Park Press, Baltimore.

Mitch, P. S., McGrady, A. and Iannone, A. (1976) Autogenic feedback training in migraine: A treatment report, *Headache*, **15**, 267–70.

Mroczek. N., Halpern, D. and McHugh, R. (1978) Electromyographic feedback and physical therapy for neuromuscular retraining in hemiplegia, *Archives of Physical Medicine and Rehabilitation*, **59**, 258–67.

Mullinix, J., Norton, B., Hack, S. and Fishman, M. (1978) Skin temperature biofeedback and migraine, *Headache*, **17**, 242–4.

Nunes, J. S. and Marks, I. M. (1975) Feedback of true heart rate during exposure *in vivo*, *Archives of General Psychiatry*, **32**, 933–60.

Obrist, P. A. (1976) The cardiovascular-behavioral interaction – as it appears today, *Psychophysiology*, **13**, 95–107.

Olton, D. S. and Noonberg, A. R. (1980) *Biofeedback: Clinical applications in behavioral medicine*, Prentice–Hall, Englewood Cliffs, New Jersey.

Patel, C. H. (1975) Twelve-month follow-up of yoga and biofeedback in the management of hypertension, *Lancet*, **i**, 62–4.

Patel, C., Marmot, M. G. and Terry, D. J. (1981) Controlled trial of biofeedback-aided behavioural methods in reducing mild hypertension, *British Medical Journal*, **282**, 2005–8.

Patel, C. H. and North, W. R. S. (1975) Randomized controlled trial of yoga and biofeedback in management of hypertension, *Lancet*, **ii**, 93–5.

Peck, C. L. and Kraft, G. H. (1977) Electromyographic biofeedback for pain related to muscle tension: Study of tension headache, back and jaw pain, *Archives of Surgery*, **112**, 889–95.

Peper, E. (1973) Frontiers of clinical biofeedback, in L. Birk (ed), *Seminars in Psychiatry*, *Vol 5*, Grune & Stratton, New York.

Philips, C. (1977) The modification of tension headache pain using EMG biofeedback, *Behaviour Research and Therapy*, **15**, 119–29.

Philips, C. (1978) A psychological analysis of tension headache, in S. J. Rachman (ed), *Contributions to medical psychology*, Pergamon Press, Oxford and New York.

Pickering, T. and Gorham, G. (1975) Learned heart rate control by a patient with a ventricular parasystolic rhythm, *Lancet*, **i**, 252–3.

Pickering, T. and Miller, N. E. (1977) Learned voluntary control of heart rate and rhythm in two subjects with premature ventricular contractions, *British Heart Journal*, **39**, 152–9.

Prigatano, G. P. and Johnson, H. J. (1972) Biofeedback control and heart rate variability to phobic stimuli: A new approach to treating spider phobia, in *Proceedings of the Annual Convention, American Psychological Association*, American Psychological Association, Washington, D.C.

Quy, R. J., Hutt, S. J. and Forrest, D. (1979) Sensorimotor rhythm feedback training and epilepsy: Some methodological and conceptual issues, *Biological Psychology*, **9**, 129–49.

Rachman, S. J. and Philips, C. (1978) *Psychology and medicine*, Penguin, Harmondsworth.

Raskin, M., Johnson, G. and Rondestvedt, T. (1973) Chronic anxiety treated by feedback-induced muscle relaxation, *Archives of General Psychiatry*, **28**, 263–6.

Reading, C. and Mohr, P. D. (1976) Biofeedback control of migraine: A pilot study, *British Journal of Social and Clinical Psychology*, **15**, 429–33.

Reeves, J. L. (1976) EMG-biofeedback reduction of tension headache: A cognitive skills training approach, *Biofeedback and Self-regulation*, **1**, 217–25.

Reeves, J. L. and Mealiea, W. (1975) Biofeedback – assisted-controlled relaxation for the treatment of flight phobias, *Journal of Behavior Therapy and Experimental Psychiatry*, **6**, 105–9.

Reinking, R. H. and Hutchings, D. (1981) Follow-up to 'Tension headaches: What form of therapy is most effective?' *Biofeedback and Self-regulation*, **6**, 57–62.

Rouse, L., Peterson, J. and Shapiro, G. (1975) EEG alpha entrainment reaction within the biofeedback setting and some possible effects on epilepsy, *Physiological Psychology*, **3**, 113–22.

Sainsbury, P. and Gibson, J. G. (1954) Symptoms of anxiety and tension and the accompanying physiological changes in the muscular system, *Journal of Neurology, Neurosurgery and Psychiatry*, **17**, 216–24.

Sargent, J. D., Green, E. E. and Walters, E. D. (1972) The use of autogenic feedback in a pilot study of migraine and tension headache, *Headache*, **12**, 120–5.

Sargent, J. D., Green, E. E. and Walters, E. D. (1973) Preliminary report on the use of autogenic feedback training in the treatment of migraine and tension headaches, *Psychosomatic Medicine*, **35**, 129–35.

Sargent, J. D., Walters, E. D. and Green, E. E. (1973) Psychosomatic self-regulation of migraine headaches, in L. Birk (ed), *Biofeedback: Behavioral medicine*, Grune & Stratton, New York.

Schachter, S. (1966) The interaction of cognitive and physiological determinants of emotional state, in C. D. Speilberger (ed), *Anxiety and behavior*, Academic Press, New York.

Schachter, S. (1971) *Emotion, obesity and crime*, Academic Press, New York.

Schwartz, G. E. (1972) Clinical applications of biofeedback: Some theoretical issues, in D. Upper and D. S. Goodenough (eds), *Behavior modification with the individual patient: Proceedings of the third annual Brockton symposium on behavior therapy*, Roche, Nutley, New Jersey.

Schwartz, G. E. (1973) Biofeedback as therapy: Some theoretical and practical issues, *American Psychologist*, **28**, 666–73.

Schwartz, G. E. and Shapiro, D. (1973) Biofeedback and essential hypertension: current findings and theoretical concerns, in L. Birk (ed), *Biofeedback: Behavioral medicine*, Grune & Stratton, New York.

Scott, R. W., Blanchard, E. B., Edmundson, E. D. and Young, L. D. (1973) A shaping procedure for heart-rate control in chronic tachycardia, *Perceptual and Motor Skills*, **37**, 327–38.

Scott, R. W., Peters, R. D., Gillespie, W, J., Blanchard, E. B., Edmundson, E. D. and Young, L. D. (1973) The use of shaping and reinforcement in the operant acceleration and deceleration of heart rate, *Behaviour Research and Therapy*, **11**, 179–85.

Seifert, A. R. and Lubar, J. F. (1975) Reduction of epileptic seizures through EEG biofeedback training, *Biological Psychology*, **3**, 157–84.

Shapiro, D., Tursky, B., Gershon, E. and Stern, M. (1969)

Effects of feedback and reinforcement on control of human systolic blood pressure, *Science*, **163**, 588–9.

Shapiro, D., Tursky, B. and Schwartz, G. E. (1970) Control of blood pressure in man by operant conditioning, *Circulation Research*, **26**, 27–32 (supplement 1).

Shapiro, D. Mainardi, J. A. and Surwit, R. S. (1977) Biofeedback and self-regulation in essential hypertension, in G. E. Schwartz and J. Beatty (eds), *Biofeedback: Theory and research*, Academic Press, New York.

Shoemaker, J. E. and Tasto, D. L. (1975) The effects of muscle relaxation on blood pressure of essential hypertensives, *Behaviour Research and Therapy*, **13**, 29–43.

Silver, B. V., Blanchard, E. B., Williamson, D. A., Theobald, D. E. and Brown, D. A. (1979) Temperature biofeedback and relaxation training in the treatment of migraine headaches: one year follow-up, *Biofeedback and Self-regulation*, **4**, 359–66.

Sirota, A. D., Schwartz, G. E. and Shapiro, D. (1974) Voluntary control of human heart rate: Effect on reaction to aversive stimulation, *Journal of Abnormal Psychology*, **83**, 261–7.

Sirota, A. D., Schwartz, G. E. and Shapiro, D. (1976) Voluntary control of human heart rate: Effect on reaction to aversive stimulation: A replication and extension, *Journal of Abnormal Psychology*, **85**, 473–7.

Solbach, P. and Sargent, J. (1977) A follow-up evaluation of the Menninger pilot migraine study using thermal training, *Headache*, **17**, 198–202.

Stephens, J. H., Harris, A. H., Brady, J. V. and Shaffer, J. W. (1975) Psychological and physiological variables associated with large magnitude voluntary heart rate changes, *Psychophysiology*, **12**, 381–7.

Sterman, M. B. (1973) Neurophysiologic and clinical studies of sensorimotor EEG biofeedback training: Some effects on epilepsy, in L. Birk (ed), *Biofeedback: Behavioral Medicine*, Grune & Stratton, New York.

Sterman, M. B. and Friar, L. (1972) Suppression of seizures in an epileptic following sensorimotor EEG feedback training, *Electroencephalography and Clinical Neurophysiology*, **33**, 89–95.

Sterman, M. B. and Macdonald, L. R. (1978) Effects of central cortical EEG feedback training on seizure incidence in poorly controlled epileptics, *Epilepsia*, **19**, 207–22.

Sterman, M. B., Macdonald, L. R. and Stone, R. F. (1974)

Biofeedback training of the sensorimotor EEG rhythm in man: Effects on epilepsy, *Epilepsia*, **15**, 395–416.

Sunderman, R. and Delk, J. (1978) Treatment of Raynaud's disease with temperature biofeedback, *Southern Medical Journal*, **71**, 340–2.

Surwit, R. S. (1973) Biofeedback: A possible treatment for Raynaud's disease, in L. Birk (ed), *Biofeedback: Behavioral medicine*, Grune & Stratton, New York.

Surwit, R. S., Pilon, R. N. and Fenton, C. H. (1978) Behavioral treatment of Raynaud's disease, *Journal of Behavioral Medicine*, **1**, 323–35.

Surwit, R. S., Shapiro, D. and Good, M. I. (1978) Comparison of cardiovascular biofeedback and meditation in the treatment of borderline essential hypertension, *Journal of Consulting and Clinical Psychology*, **46**, 252–63.

Tarchanoff, J. R. (1885) Über die Willkurliche Acceleration der Herzschlage beim Menschen, *Pfluger's Archive der gesamten Physiologie*, **35**, 109–35.

Taub, E. (1977) Self-regulation of human tissue temperature, in G. E. Schwartz and J. Beatty (eds), *Biofeedback: Theory and research*, Academic Press, New York.

Townsend, R. E., House, J. F. and Addario, D. (1975) A comparison of EMG feedback and progressive muscle relaxation training in anxiety neurosis, *American Journal of Psychiatry*, **132**, 598–601.

Tunis, M. M. and Wolff, H. G. (1954) Studies on headache: Cranial artery vasoconstriction and muscle contraction headache, *Archives of Neurology and Psychiatry*, **71**, 425–34.

Turin, A. and Johnson, W. G. (1976) Biofeedback therapy for migraine headaches, *Archives of General Psychiatry*, **33**, 517–9.

Valins, S. (1966) Cognitive effects of false heart-rate feedback, *Journal of Personality and Social Psychology*, **4**, 400–8.

Victor, R., Mainardi, J. A. and Shapiro, D. (1978) Effects of biofeedback and voluntary control procedures on heart rate and perception of pain during the cold pressor test, *Psychosomatic Medicine*, **40**, 216–25.

Walsh, P., Dale, A. and Anderson, D. E. (1977) Comparison of biofeedback pulse wave velocity and progressive relaxation in essential hypertensives, *Perceptual and Motor Skills*, **44**, 839–43.

Waters, W. E. (1970) Community studies of the prevalence of headache, *Headache*, **9**, 178–86.

Waters, W, E. (1974) The Pontypridd headache survey, *Headache*, **14**, 81–90.

Weiss, T. and Engel, B. T. (1971) Operant conditioning of heart rate in patients with premature ventricular contractions, *Psychosomatic Medicine*, **33**, 301–21.

West, H. F. and Savage, W. F. (1918) Voluntary acceleration of the heart beat, *Archives of International Medicine*, **22**, 290–5.

Wickramasekera, I. (1972a) Electromyographic feedback training and tension headaches: Preliminary observations, *American Journal of Clinical Hypnosis*, **15**, 83–5.

Wickramasekera, I. (1972b) Instructions and EMG feedback in systematic desensitization: A case report, *Behavior Therapy*, **3**, 460–5.

Wickramasekera, I. (1973a) Temperature feedback for the control of migraine, *Journal of Behavior Therapy and Experimental Psychiatry*, **4**, 343–5.

Wickramasekera, I. (1973b) The application of verbal instructions and EMG feedback to the management of tension headache – Preliminary observations, *Headache*, **13**, 74–6.

Wickramasekera, I. (1974) Heart rate feedback and the management of cardiac neurosis, *Journal of Abnormal Psychology*, **83**, 578–80.

Wickramasekera, I. (1976) On the apparent intrusion of a recurring nightmare into an EMG feedback training procedure, in I. Wickramasekera (ed), *Biofeedback, behavior therapy and hypnosis: Potentiating the verbal control of behavior for clinicians*, Nelson, London.

Wooldridge, C. P. and Russell, G. (1976) Head position training with the cerebral palsied child: An application of biofeedback techniques, *Archives of Physical Medicine and Rehabilitation*, **57**, 407–14.

Wyler, A. R., Lockard, J. S., Ward, A. A. Jr. and Finch, C. A. (1976) Conditioned EEG desensitization and seizure occurrence in patients, *Electroencephalography and Clinical Neurophysiology*, **41**, 501–12.

Index